CPCU 530 Course Guide

Business Law for Insurance Professionals
1st Edition

The Institutes
720 Providence Road, Suite 100
Malvern, Pennsylvania 19355-3433

1st Edition • 3rd Printing • November 2013

ISBN 978-0-89463-432-1

Contents

Study Materials iii

Student Resources iv

Using This Course Guide iv

1. Introduction to U.S. Law 1.1

2. Contract Law 2.1

3. Contract Law: Insurance Applications 3.1

4. Commercial Law 4.1

5. Property Law 5.1

6. Tort Law 6.1

7. Agency Law 7.1

8. Agency Law: Insurance Applications 8.1

9. Employment Law and Business Entities 9.1

10. The International Legal Environment 10.1

Exam Information 1

Canons of the CPCU Code of Professional Conduct 5

 ## Study Materials Available for CPCU 530

Business Law for Insurance Professionals, 1st ed., 2010, AICPCU.

CPCU 530 *Course Guide*, 1st ed., 2010, AICPCU (includes access codes for SMART Online Practice Exams).

CPCU 530 SMART Study Aids—Review Notes and Flash Cards, 1st ed.

Student Resources

Catalog A complete listing of our offerings can be found in *Succeed*, The Institutes' professional development catalog, including information about:

- Current programs and courses
- Current textbooks, course guides, SMART Study Aids, and online offerings
- Program completion requirements
- Exam registration

To obtain a copy of the catalog, visit our website at www.TheInstitutes.org or contact Customer Service at (800) 644-2101.

How to Prepare for Institutes Exams This free handbook is designed to help you by:

- Giving you ideas on how to use textbooks and course guides as effective learning tools
- Providing steps for answering exam questions effectively
- Recommending exam-day strategies

The handbook is printable from the Student Services Center on The Institutes' website at www.TheInstitutes.org or available by calling Customer Service at (800) 644-2101.

Educational Counseling Services To ensure that you take courses matching both your needs and your skills, you can obtain free counseling from The Institutes by:

- Emailing your questions to advising@TheInstitutes.org
- Calling an Institutes' counselor directly at (610) 644-2100, ext. 7601
- Obtaining and completing a self-inventory form, available on our website at www.TheInstitutes.org or by contacting Customer Service at (800) 644-2101

Exam Registration Information As you proceed with your studies, be sure to arrange for your exam.

- Visit our website at www.TheInstitutes.org/forms to access and print the Registration Booklet, which contains information and forms needed to register for your exam.
- Plan to register with The Institutes well in advance of your exam.

How to Contact The Institutes For more information on any of these publications and services:

- Visit our website at www.TheInstitutes.org
- Call us at (800) 644-2101 or (610) 644-2100 outside the U.S.
- Email us at customerservice@TheInstitutes.org
- Fax us at (610) 640-9576
- Write to us at The Institutes, Customer Service, 720 Providence Road, Suite 100, Malvern, PA 19355-3433

Using This Course Guide

This course guide will help you learn the course content and prepare for the exam.

Each assignment in this course guide typically includes the following components:

Educational Objectives These are the most important study tools in the course guide. Because all of the questions on the exam are based on the Educational Objectives, the best way to study for the exam is to focus on these objectives.

Each Educational Objective typically begins with one of the following action words, which indicate the level of understanding required for the exam:

Analyze—Determine the nature and the relationship of the parts.

Apply—Put to use for a practical purpose.

Associate—Bring together into relationship.

Calculate—Determine numeric values by mathematical process.

Classify—Arrange or organize according to class or category.

Compare—Show similarities and differences.

Contrast—Show only differences.

Define—Give a clear, concise meaning.

Describe—Represent or give an account.

Determine—Settle or decide.

Evaluate—Determine the value or merit.

Explain—Relate the importance or application.

Identify or list—Name or make a list.

Illustrate—Give an example.

Justify—Show to be right or reasonable.

Paraphrase—Restate in your own words.

Recommend—Suggest or endorse something to be used.

Summarize—Concisely state the main points.

Outline The outline lists the topics in the assignment. Read the outline before the required reading to become familiar with the assignment content and the relationships of topics.

Key Words and Phrases These words and phrases are fundamental to understanding the assignment and have a common meaning for those working in insurance. After completing the required reading, test your understanding of the assignment's Key Words and Phrases by writing their definitions.

Review Questions The review questions test your understanding of what you have read. Review the Educational Objectives and required reading, then answer the questions to the best of your ability. When you are finished, check the answers at the end of the assignment to evaluate your comprehension.

Application Questions These questions continue to test your knowledge of the required reading by applying what you've studied to "hypothetical" real-life situations. Again, check the suggested answers at the end of the assignment to review your progress.

Sample Exam Your course guide includes a sample exam (located at the back) or a code for accessing SMART Online Practice Exams (which appears on the inside of the cover). Use the option available for the course you're taking to become familiar with the test format.

For courses that offer SMART Online Practice Exams, you can either download and print a sample credentialing exam or take full practice exams using questions like those that will appear on your credentialing exam. SMART Online Practice Exams are as close as you can get to experiencing an actual exam before taking one.

More Study Aids

The Institutes also produce supplemental study tools, called SMART Study Aids, for many of our courses. When SMART Study Aids are available for a course, they are listed on page iii of the course guide. SMART Study Aids include Review Notes and Flash Cards and are excellent tools to help you learn and retain the information in each assignment.

Direct Your Learning

1

Introduction to U.S. Law

Educational Objectives

After learning the content of this assignment, you should be able to:

1. Describe the U.S. civil-law and common-law systems and classifications.

2. Describe the role and usual characteristics of each of the following sources of U.S. law:

   - Constitutions

   - Legislative bodies

   - Courts

   - Executive branches

   - Administrative agencies

3. Describe the steps, motions, rules, and other concepts involved in pretrial procedures, trial procedures, and appeals.

4. Describe each of these alternative dispute resolution procedures:

   - Arbitration

   - Mediation

   - Negotiation

5. Describe these aspects of administrative agency procedures:

   - Rulemaking function

   - Adjudicatory function

   - Investigative powers

   - Judicial review

Outline

▶ **The U.S. Legal System**
   A. Civil-Law System — *codes of written laws or statutes*
   B. Common-Law System — *derived from court decisions*
      1. Judicial Influence on Common Law
      2. The Evolution of Common Law — *changes through landmark decisions - historic court cases*
      3. Equity
   C. Classifications of U.S. Law
      1. Classification as Criminal or Civil Law
      2. Classification by Subject Matter
      3. Classification as Substantive or Procedural Law

▶ **Sources of U.S. Law**
   A. Constitutions
      1. Separation of Powers
      2. Provisions Relevant to Insurance
   B. Legislative Bodies
   C. Courts — *judicial*
      1. Federal Court System
      2. State Court Systems
   D. Executive Branches
   E. Administrative Agencies

▶ **Civil Trial Procedures**
   A. Pretrial Procedure
   B. Trial Procedure
   C. Appeals

▶ **Alternative Dispute Resolution**
   A. Arbitration
   B. Mediation
   C. Negotiation

▶ **Administrative Agency Procedures**
   A. Role of Administrative Agencies
   B. Agencies' Rulemaking Function
   C. Agencies' Adjudicatory Function
   D. Agencies' Investigative Powers
   E. Judicial Review

s.m.a.r.t. tips

Don't spend time on material you have already mastered. The SMART Review Notes are organized by the Educational Objectives found in each assignment to help you track your study.

For each assignment, you should define or describe each of the Key Words and Phrases and answer each of the Review and Application Questions.

Educational Objective 1
Describe the U.S. civil-law and common-law systems and classifications.

Key Words and Phrases

Doctrine of stare decisis

"to stand by things decided" - lower courts must follow precedents set by higher courts

Equity

fairness - body of principles constituting what is fair and right

Criminal law

imposes penalties for wrongdoings against society

Civil law

applies to legal matters not governed by criminal law

Substantive law

creates, defines, regulates parties' rights, duties, and powers

Procedural law

prescribes the steps for enforcing the rights and duties defined by substantive law

Review Questions

1-1. Describe the civil-law and common-law systems.

civil-law — have comprehensive codes of written laws, that apply to all legal questions

common-law — body of law derived from court decisions

1-2. Explain how the common law changes.

court can find a prior decision clearly wrong and discard it as precedent; new laws may also be passed; also changes through landmark court decisions, historic court rulings

1-3. Distinguish between civil and criminal law.

Criminal — applies to acts the society deems so harmful to public welfare that gov't is responsible for prosecuting and punishing
  - burden of proof is beyond a reasonable doubt

civil — applies to legal matters that are not governed by criminal law
  - burden of proof is by a preponderance of evidence (more weight for decision vs. not for decision)

Application Question

1-4. In 1852, the Midvale Township court wrote an opinion stating that if a dog bites a person, the dog's owner must pay for the damages resulting from the dog bite, whatever the circumstances. In 1875, Midvale Township passed a law saying that any owner of a dog who allows that dog to run free is responsible for any damage the dog causes. In 1952, the local court wrote an opinion saying that dogs owned by green-eyed people could have "one free bite" unless the dog has shown vicious propensities. That is, if a dog bites a person for the first time, its green-eyed owner is not liable unless the dog previously had shown vicious propensities. However, upon the second bite, the dog owner with green eyes is liable. Mary, who has brown eyes, lives in Midvale. Her large dog, Sam, which had never shown any vicious propensities but had knocked a few people down, just bit Mary's neighbor. The neighbor is suing Mary. Describe how the common law applies here.

- She would be responsible since all laws
  supplement the prior ones

Educational Objective 2

Describe the role and usual characteristics of each of the following sources of U.S. law:

- **Constitutions**
- **Legislative bodies**
- **Courts**
- **Executive branches**
- **Administrative agencies**

Key Words and Phrases

Equal Protection Clause

part of 14th amendment - prohibits state laws that
discriminate unfairly and requires equal treatment

National Association of Insurance Commissioners (NAIC)

pools information to help regulators coordinate
responses to changing conditions in the insurance
marketplace
also develops model laws, regulations, and guidelines ▶▶

Original jurisdiction

Courts in which cases are initiated

Diversity jurisdiction

the authority of federal district courts to hear cases involving parties from different states

Writ of certiorari

a request for the Supreme Court to consider a case

Conflicts of law

a body of law that resolves questions when states' laws conflict

Administrative law

Agency rules, regulations, and rulings have the full force of law

Review Questions

2-1.   Describe the provisions of the U.S. Constitution relevant to the insurance business.

— delegation of powers to Congress: to regulate commerce, levy and collect taxes, borrow money, and to est. uniform laws on bankruptcy
— Commerce clause: regulate trade w/ foreign nations and among the states
— due process clause: guarantees notice and a hearing before fed. gov't can deprive of life, liberty, property

— equal protection clause: prohibits state laws that discriminate unfairly and requires equal treatment to all

2-2.   Explain the role of the National Association of Insurance Commissioners (NAIC) in promoting uniformity in the states' regulation of insurance.

pools information to help regulators coordinate responses to changing conditions in the insurance marketplace
also develops model laws, regulations, and guidelines

2-3. Discuss how administrative agencies become sources of law.

agency rules, regulations, and rulings have full force of law — legislative delegation of rulemaking power to an administrative agency is considered constitutional as long as ① the legislation carefully defines the scope of the delegated power ② the agency exercises its rulemaking power w/in the defined scope, ③ the rules are subject to court review

Educational Objective 3
Describe the steps, motions, rules, and other concepts involved in pretrial procedures, trial procedures, and appeals.

Key Words and Phrases

Allegation

claim made in a complaint by the plaintiff (what they're expecting to prove)

Complaint

allegations made by a plaintiff in a lawsuit

Pleading

formal written statement of the facts and claims of each party

Cause of action

plaintiff's legal grounds to sue a defendant

Answer

document filed in court by defendant responding to plaintiff's complaint

Counterclaim

a complaint brought by a defendant against the plaintiff

▶▶

Motion

> formal request for court to take a
> particular action

Motion to dismiss

> request that a court terminate an action
> because of settlement, voluntary w/drawal,
> or procedural defect

Motion for summary judgment

> pretrial request asking court to enter a
> judgment when no material facts are
> in dispute

Discovery

> pretrial exchange of all relevant info btween
> plaintiff and defendant

Deposition

> pretrial discovery tool involving oral
> examination of a witness

Interrogatories

> specific written questions or requests
> raised by one party

Subpoena

> legal order to a witness to appear to
> testify or produce documents

Direct examination

> questioning one's own witness

Cross-examination

> questioning an opposing party

Relevance

> a quality of evidence that suggests the evidence
> is more or less likely to be true

Materiality

a quality of evidence that tends to establish a particular element of the claim that has legal significance

Competence

a quality of evidence that suggests the source is reliable and the evidence is adequate to justify admission in court

Hearsay rule

prevents the admission of out-of-court statements not made under oath by a person who is unavailable to testify

General verdict

entails a complete finding and a single conclusion by a jury on all issues presented

Special verdict

makes findings of fact by answering specific questions posed by the judge - the judge then applies the law to the facts as the jury has found them

Res judicata

"claim preclusion" - prevents parties from raising, in a subsequent lawsuit, issues or facts that could have been, but were not, included in the 1st lawsuit

Review Questions

3-1.   Identify the filing parties and the purpose of the complaint and the answer in a lawsuit.

- plaintiff files the complaint - it sets out plaintiff's allegations, explains why plaintiff has cause of action against defendant, and states the remedy requested
- defendant files an answer to the complaint - includes counter claims and why plaintiff shouldn't win - may also include entry of appearance which means defendant will appear in court

3-2.   Explain the purpose of pretrial discovery and some of the tools used during discovery.

- tools include depositions, interrogatories, subpoenas, and motions to compel compliance w/ discovery requests
- enables parties to know as much as possible before ▶▶ trial and prevents surprises - can sometimes lead to settlement

3-3. Discuss the three requirements for evidence presented during a trial.

— must have relevance (more or less true)

— must be material (legal significance)

— must have competence (source is reliable)

3-4. Contrast two different decisions an appellate court might render regarding improper evidence presented at trial

— can send case back to lower court for new trial

— or determine that evidence didn't prejudice the appellant

Educational Objective 4

Describe each of these alternative dispute resolution procedures:

- **Arbitration**
- **Mediation**
- **Negotiation**

Key Words and Phrases

Alternative dispute resolution (ADR)

procedures to help settle disputes w/out litigation, including arbitration, mediation, and negotiation
(binding)   (nonbinding)

Mediation

disputing parties use a neutral ~~party~~ outside party to examine the issues and develop a mutually agreeable settlement (nonbinding)

Review Questions

4-1. When is alternative dispute resolution (ADR) binding on parties?

When the parties have agreed in advance that it will be binding

4-2. Explain the role of the mediator in alternative dispute resolution.

neutral 3rd party who acts as a catalyst to help parties analyze their dispute, consider possible solutions, and devise a compromise formula

4-3. Explain how mini-trials and court-sponsored mock summary jury trials can lead to negotiation of major disputes.

- lawyers or others present evidence and arguments to panel - neutral party acts as mediator or issues an advisory opinion after evidence and arguments
- presents issues to both parties in a dispute, so it can encourage negotiation and settlement

---

Educational Objective 5

Describe these aspects of administrative agency procedures:

- **Rulemaking function**
- **Adjudicatory function**
- **Investigative powers**
- **Judicial review**

Key Words and Phrases

Legislative rule

Come from a statutory delegation of authority and have the same force as a law enacted by Congress or a legislature

Interpretative rule

interpret statutes, providing guidance for agency staff or regulated parties

Procedural rule

primarily internal

prescribe procedures for agency operations, for legislative rulemaking, and for adjudication proceedings

Standing to sue

must show that the rule or its application would impair or interfere w/ that party's legal rights and privileges

Final order

the basis of appeal — final conclusion or disposition

Exhaustion of administrative remedies

completion of all possible administrative procedures and appeals in a case

Review Questions

5-1. List the three types of administrative agency rules.

1) legislative
2) interpretive
3) procedural

5-2. What actions can an administrative agency take after it has reviewed all comments about a proposed rule?

- adopt the originally proposed rule

- make minimal or extensive changes

- nullify the proposed rule

5-3. What must be included in an appropriate notice for an administrative agency adjudicatory proceeding?

- Statement of hearing time, place, nature
- Statement of hearing's legal authority + jurisdiction
- reference to the particular statute or rule involved
- short, clear statement of the matters at issue

5-4. Describe the United States constitutional limitations on agency investigations.

- protection against unreasonable searches + seizures (4th amendment)
- protection against self-incrimination (5th amendment)

5-5. What is required before courts will review administrative agency decisions?

- must have standing to sue
- final order has been issued
- doctrine of exhaustion of administrative remedies has been satisfied

Application Question

5-6. The Board of Health, an administrative agency with rulemaking authority, adopted, without a formal hearing, a rule prohibiting tattooing by any unlicensed person. The rule, which was made final, was based on the opinion of medical experts on the Board of Health staff asserting a definite connection between tattooing and hepatitis. Several unlicensed persons who had been operating tattoo parlors sued to have the rule declared invalid.

a. Explain whether the unlicensed tattoo-parlor operators must seek further administrative action before appealing to the courts.

- must go before board first and exhaust all administrative remedies

b. Explain whether the unlicensed tattoo-parlor operators have standing to sue and a right to appeal.

- rule directly and ~~addresses~~ adversely affects them

c. Did the adoption of the rule affect the unlicensed tattoo-parlor operators' constitutional rights in any way? Explain.

- can allege their property (earnings, shops) was taken away w/out due process of law

Answers to Assignment 1 Questions

NOTE: These answers are provided to give students a basic understanding of acceptable types of responses. They often are not the only valid answers and are not intended to provide an exhaustive response to the questions.

Educational Objective 1

1-1. A civil-law system has a comprehensive code of written laws or statutes. A common-law system is a body of law derived from court decisions as opposed to statutes or constitutions.

1-2. Common law changes through court examination of precedent. A court may apply a precedent to new cases or discard it if it has lost its usefulness, or it may make landmark decisions that depart from precedent.

1-3. Criminal law applies to acts society deems so harmful to the public welfare that government is responsible for prosecuting and punishing the perpetrators. Civil law applies to legal matters that are not governed by criminal law, protecting rights and providing remedies for breaches of duties owed to others.

1-4. The original court case in 1852 was the law in Midvale Township and provided that a dog owner must pay damages for any bite. The 1875 statutory law added to the case law by providing that, in addition to damages for bites, a dog owner must pay for any damage caused by a dog running free. The 1952 court case eliminated damages for first bites of dogs owned by green-eyed people only. In summary, each of these laws supplemented the others and did not overrule them. The township also could have legally passed statutory law changing case law.

Educational Objective 2

2-1. The Constitution delegates powers to Congress to regulate commerce, levy and collect taxes, borrow money, and establish uniform laws on bankruptcy. Congress thus has implied powers to pass laws necessary to implement the powers expressly delegated. The Constitution's Commerce Clause gives Congress the power to regulate commerce with foreign nations and among the states, including insurance. The Fifth Amendment's Due Process Clause guarantees notice and a hearing before the federal government can deprive any person of life, liberty, or property. The Fourteenth Amendment extends the same protection in state government actions, which can give rise to a complaint by an insurer if the state changes a premium rate without giving sufficient notice to the insurer. The Fourteenth Amendment's Equal Protection Clause also prohibits state laws that discriminate unfairly and protects both individuals and corporations.

2-2. The NAIC pools information to help regulators coordinate responses to changing conditions in the insurance marketplace. The NAIC also develops model laws, regulations, and guidelines.

2-3. Agency rules, regulations, and rulings have the full force of law and constitute the body of administrative law. The legislative delegation of rulemaking power to an administrative agency is constitutional as long as the legislation carefully defines the scope of the delegated power, the agency exercises its rulemaking power within the defined scope, and the rules are subject to judicial review.

Educational Objective 3

3-1. The party who files the complaint is the plaintiff. The complaint is the first pleading filed with the court. The complaint sets out the plaintiff's allegations, explains why the plaintiff has a cause of action, and states what remedy the plaintiff requests. The complaint also tells the court why it has jurisdiction over the matter.

The defendant must file the answer to the complaint within the length of time specified in the summons that accompanies the complaint. The answer responds to the plaintiff's complaint and explains why the plaintiff should not win the case. The answer may include counterclaims. It can also include only an entry of appearance, which neither admits nor denies any allegations in the complaint and states only that the defendant will appear in court.

3-2. The purpose of discovery is for lawyers on both sides to gather as much information as possible about all allegations and evidence the parties might present. Discovered information enables the parties to know as much as possible before trial and prevents surprises. If testimony at trial contradicts information obtained during discovery, lawyers can use the pretrial evidence to challenge the evidence presented at trial. Discovery can sometimes lead to settlement once the parties know all the evidence. Some discovery tools include depositions, interrogatories, and subpoenas.

3-3. Evidence must have relevance to the case. For example, evidence regarding an insurance policy is not relevant to determining whether the insured was negligent in an accident. Evidence must also be material. A fact can be relevant but not material. For example, the make and model of a car in an accident is immaterial unless there was a physical defect in that model that caused or contributed to the accident. The evidence must have competence. For example, hearsay or expert witness evidence may not be competent.

3-4. If an appellate court finds that the trial court improperly admitted evidence that was prejudicial, or harmful, to the appellant's case, the court can send the case back to the lower court for a new trial. However, an appellate court might determine that the evidence, although improperly admitted at trial, did not prejudice the appellant.

Educational Objective 4

4-1. ADR can be binding on parties when they have agreed in advance that it will be binding.

4-2. The mediator is a neutral third party who acts as a catalyst to help parties analyze their dispute, consider possible solutions, and devise a compromise formula.

4-3. In a mini-trial, lawyers or others familiar with the dispute present evidence and arguments to a panel that may include business executives or other professionals. A neutral party, such as a retired judge or another expert, can act as mediator or issue an advisory opinion after the presentation of evidence and arguments. Because the mini-trial presents the issues to both parties in a dispute, it can encourage negotiation and settlement. Summary jury trials are brief mock trials before juries. The parties can accept the jury's advisory verdict, or the verdict can provide the basis for further negotiations toward settlement.

Educational Objective 5

5-1. The three types of administrative agency rules are these:

- Legislative rules

- Interpretative rules

- Procedural rules

5-2. After reviewing comments about a proposed rule, an agency can take one of these actions:

- Adopt the originally proposed rule

- Make minimal or extensive changes to the rule

- Nullify the proposed rule

5-3. These items must be included in an appropriate notice for an administrative agency adjudicatory proceeding:

- A statement of the hearing time, place, and nature

- A statement of the hearing's legal authority and jurisdiction

- Reference to the statute or rule involved

- A short, clear statement of the matters at issue

5-4. The U.S. Constitution places these limitations on agency investigations:

- Fourth Amendment protection against unreasonable searches and seizures

- Fifth Amendment protection against self-incrimination

5-5. To take an administrative action to a court for judicial review, these must have occurred:

- The plaintiff must have standing to sue.

- The agency must have issued a final order in the case.

- The plaintiff must have exhausted all administrative remedies.

5-6. These answers apply to the Board of Health ruling questions:

a. The complainants first should exhaust all administrative remedies. No court will hear the case without the complainants' first having challenged the rule before the Board of Health under administrative procedures.

b. Because the new rule applies directly to and adversely affects unlicensed persons who operate tattoo parlors, and because these complainants are unlicensed persons who operate tattoo parlors, they have standing to sue.

c. The tattoo-parlor operators can allege that their property (earnings, shops) was taken away without due process of law.

Direct Your Learning

Contract Law

Educational Objectives

After learning the content of this assignment, you should be able to:

1. Contrast the following types of contracts:
   - Bilateral and unilateral
   - Executed and executory
   - Express and implied
   - Void and voidable

2. Describe the requirements of a valid offer.

3. Describe the requirements of a valid acceptance.

4. Describe the circumstances in which each of the following has the capacity to contract:
   - Minor
   - Insane person
   - Intoxicated person
   - Artificial entity

5. Describe consideration for a contract in terms of the following:
   - Types of consideration
   - Situations in which a contract is enforceable despite a lack of consideration

6. Given a contract, determine whether it has a legal purpose.

7. Explain how each of the following may render a contract unenforceable:
   - Fraud
   - Mistake
   - Duress

2

- Undue influence

- Innocent misrepresentation

- Statute of frauds

- Parol evidence rule

8. Paraphrase the rules on contract construction that courts commonly use to interpret contracts.

9. Describe the circumstances in which a third party would have enforceable rights under a contract.

10. Describe the various ways in which the contractual obligations of the parties to a contract can be terminated.

11. Describe breach of contract in terms of the following:

- Types of breach

- Remedies for breach

12. Given a case, determine whether a described contract would be legally enforceable.

Outline

▶ **Types of Contracts**
  A. Bilateral and Unilateral Contracts
  B. Executed and Executory Contracts
  C. Express and Implied Contracts
  D. Voidable Contracts and Void Contracts

▶ **Requirements of an Offer**
  A. Intent to Contract
  B. Definite Terms
  C. Communication to Offeree
  D. Duration and Termination
    1. Lapse of Time
    2. Operation of Law
    3. Offeree's Rejection
    4. Counteroffers
    5. Offeror's Revocation

▶ **Requirements of a Valid Acceptance**
  A. Acceptance by Offeree
  B. Unconditional and Unequivocal Acceptance
  C. Offeree's Communication of Acceptance

▶ **Capacity to Contract**
  A. Competent Parties
  B. Minors' Contracts
  C. Insane Persons' Contracts
  D. Intoxicated Persons' Contracts
  E. Artificial Entities' Contracts

▶ **Consideration**
  A. Types of Consideration
    1. Valuable Consideration
    2. Forbearance
    3. Present and Future Consideration
    4. Binding Promise
  B. What Is Not Valid Consideration?
    1. Past Consideration
    2. Promise to Perform an Existing Obligation
    3. Compromise and Release of Claims
  C. Exceptions to the Consideration Requirement
    1. Promissory Estoppel
    2. Charitable Subscriptions

▶ **Legal Purpose of a Contract**
  A. Types of Illegal Contracts
    1. Contracts to Commit Crimes or Torts
    2. Contracts Harmful to the Public Interest
    3. Usury Contracts
    4. Wagering Contracts
    5. Contracts With Unlicensed Practitioners
    6. Contracts to Transfer Liability for Negligence
    7. Contracts in Restraint of Marriage
    8. Contracts in Restraint of Trade
    9. Unconscionable Bargains
  B. Exceptions to the Legal Purpose Requirement

▶ **Enforceability of a Contract**
  A. Genuine Assent
    1. Fraud
    2. Mistake
    3. Duress
    4. Undue Influence
    5. Innocent Misrepresentation
  B. Statute of Frauds and Parol Evidence Rule
    1. Statute of Frauds
    2. Parol Evidence Rule

▶ **Contract Interpretation**
  A. Plain Meaning
  B. Effectuation of Intent
  C. Entire and Divisible Contracts
  D. Clerical Errors and Omissions
  E. Contradictory Terms
  F. Ambiguity
  G. Parties' Own Interpretation
  H. Legal and Fair Interpretation
  I. Trade Usage, Course of Dealings, and Performance

▶ **Third-Party Contractual Rights**
  A. Contract Assignments
    1. Rights Assignable
    2. Rights Not Assignable
    3. Forms of Assignment
    4. Assignee's Rights

s.m.a.r.t. tips Reduce the number of Key Words and Phrases that you must review. SMART Flash Cards contain the Key Words and Phrases and their definitions, allowing you to set aside those cards that you have mastered.

Outline

　　5. Notice of Assignment

　B. Third-Party Beneficiaries

　　1. Types of Third-Party Beneficiaries

　　2. Characteristics of Beneficiary Contracts

　　3. Beneficiaries' Rights

▶ Termination of a Contract

　A. Performance

　B. Agreement of the Parties

　C. Substitution

　D. Impossibility

　E. Fraudulent Alteration

　F. Contractual Conditions

▶ Breach of Contract

　A. Types of Breach

　　1. Repudiation

　　2. Anticipatory Breach

　　3. Material Breach

　B. Remedies for Breach

　　1. Damages

　　2. Equitable Remedies

▶ Contracts Case Study

　A. Case Facts

　B. Was a Contract Formed?

　C. Is the Contract Enforceable?

　D. Was the Contract Breached, and, if so, What Is the Remedy?

For each assignment, you should define or describe each of the Key Words and Phrases and answer each of the Review and Application Questions.

Educational Objective 1

Contrast the following types of contracts:

- **Bilateral and unilateral**
- **Executed and executory**
- **Express and implied**
- **Void and voidable**

Key Words and Phrases

Contract

legally enforceable agreement btween 2 or more parties

Promisor

~~party to whom a promise is made~~

party making a promise

Promisee

party to whom a promise is made

Privity of contract

relationship that exists between the parties of a contract

Third-party beneficiary

~~has legal~~ not a party to a contract, but who benefits from it and has legal right to enforce it

Breach of contract

the failure to fulfill a contractual promise

Bilateral contract

most contracts are bilateral   *each party promizes performance*

Unilateral contract

one party makes a promise or undertakes performance

Executed contract

has been completely performed

Executory contract

not completely performed by one or both parties

Express contract

terms and intentions are explicitly stated

Implied contract

terms and intentions are indicated by actions
of parties and surrounding circumstances

Implied-in-fact contract

i.e. credit acct @ local store

not express, but parties intended that it existed

Implied-in-law contract

Quasi contracts

not actual contract, but is imposed by law
because of parties' conduct

Voidable contract

Can be rejected based on some circumstance
surrounding its execution (can also continue in force
and be executed)

Void contract

agreement that
never reaches contract status and therefore is
not legally enforceable or binding

Review Questions

1-1. Compare bilateral and unilateral contracts.

bilateral - both parties promise performance
   i.e.   Tony $\xrightarrow{paint}$ Jay agree to exchange
                    $\xleftarrow{\$500}$

unilateral - only one party promises
   i.e.   Jay $\xrightarrow{\$500}$ Tony only if Tony $\xrightarrow{paints}$ Jay

1-2. Contrast voidable and void contracts.

voidable - valid contract that can continue in
       force unless a party chooses to void it

void - contract never really created - intended
       to be a contract but never actually became one

Educational Objective 2
Describe the requirements of a valid offer.

Key Words and Phrases

Offer

requires some action by the intended recipient

Offeror

promises to give something in return for a promise
   or an act by another party

Offeree

makes a promise or acts in return for something
   offered by another party

Counteroffer

proposal made by an offeree to an offeror that
varies in some material way from the original
offer, resulting in rejection of the original offer
and constituting a new offer

▶▶

Review Questions

2-1. Describe the three requirements for an offer to be valid for contract purposes.

1) intent to contract
2) definite terms
3) communication to other party

2-2. Explain how lapse of time affects an offer for contract purposes.

- offers don't remain open indefinitely
- ceases to be binding when the time the offer specifies expires or when a reasonable amt. of time passes (if not specified)

2-3. Under what circumstances can an offeror revoke an offer?

- any time before acceptance but only effective when communicated

Educational Objective 3

Describe the requirements of a valid acceptance.

Key Words and Phrases

Acceptance

assent to an offer that occurs when party agrees to the proposal or does what has been proposed

Forbearance

the act of giving up or the promise to give up a legal right

Substantial performance

performance of primary, necessary terms of an agreement

Review Questions

3-1. Who can accept these types of offers?

    a.   An offer made to one person

only the offeree can accept.

    b.   An offer made to a group of people

any member of the group can accept

    c.   An offer made to the public

anyone can accept

3-2. Contrast acceptance of an offer with a counteroffer.

— acceptance must be unconditional and unequivocal

— if deviates from the offer's terms, it becomes a counter offer

3-3. Explain the different requirements for communication in unilateral and bilateral contracts.

> unilateral - no communication other than performance or forbearance
>
> bilateral - offeree must communicate acceptance to the offeror

---

Educational Objective 4

Describe the circumstances in which each of the following has the capacity to contract:

- **Minor**
- **Insane person**
- **Intoxicated person**
- **Artificial entity**

Key Words and Phrases

Competent party

> has basic or minimal ability to do something and the mental ability to understand problems and make decisions

Restitution

> the return of specific property by court order (minors' contracts - before avoiding a contract)

Review Questions

4-1. Explain the concept of legal capacity to contract.

> - capacity refers to one's ability to sue or be sued or to enter into an enforceable contract
> - must be able to understand the consequences of one's actions
> - considered incompetent when a person lacks legal capacity

4-2. Describe the four parties who typically lack capacity to contract.

1) minors   (underage)
2) insane persons (adjudged insane or claim insanity)
3) intoxicated persons (under the influence)
4) artificial entities (some corp have capacity, but some
       such as ins, banking, transportation
       corps are restricted)

4-3. Discuss the extent of a corporation's competence to enter into contracts.

- corps are viewed as people in the
    eyes of the law
- can enter into contracts, but may be restricted
    by its corporate charter or by license or
      regulation (such as insurers, banking, transportation)

Educational Objective 5

Describe consideration for a contract in terms of the following:

- **Types of consideration**
- **Situations in which a contract is enforceable despite a lack of consideration**

Key Words and Phrases

Consideration

Something of value or bargained for and exchanged
    by the parties to a contract

Good consideration

based on natural love or affection, or on moral duty,
    that is _not_ sufficient to support a contract

Valuable consideration

necessary and sufficient to support a valid contract

Gratuitous promise

not supported by valuable consideration and
    not binding

▶▶

examples

Accord and satisfaction

> an agreement (accord) to substitute performance other
> than that required in a contract and the carrying out
> of that agreement (satisfaction)

Promissory estoppel

> permits enforcement of a promise w/out consideration
> in order to prevent injustice

Review Questions

5-1. Describe the five types of consideration that are sufficient to form an enforceable contract.

> 1) valuable consideration
> 2) forbearance
> 3) present consideration
> 4) future consideration
> 5) binding promises

5-2. Describe three types of consideration that are insufficient for forming a binding contract.

> 1) past consideration
> 2) promises to perform existing obligations
> 3) compromise and release of claims

5-3. Discuss exceptions to the consideration requirement in contracts.

> enforceable for equitable or public policy
> reasons or because of state law exceptions
> i.e. -- promissory estoppel
>   - charitable subscriptions

Application Question

5-4. Discuss the following in a property-casualty insurance contract:

   a.   The insurer's consideration

   its promise to indemnify or pay on behalf of an insured for loss resulting from a covered occurrence

   b.   The insured's consideration

   the premium payment or the promise of premium payment

   c.   Whether prepayment of premium is necessary before coverage begins

   not a condition necessary to make a valid contract in P+C
   — insurer cannot refuse to pay based on lack of consideration

---

Educational Objective 6
Given a contract, determine whether it has a legal purpose.

Key Words and Phrases

Insurable interest

An interest that is not unduly remote and that would cause the interested party to suffer financial loss if an insured event occurred

Usury

Any contract allowing a lender more than the max. legal interest (charging an illegally high interest rate) on a loan

▶▶

Negligence

failure to exercise the degree of care that a reasonable person in a similar situation would exercise to avoid harming others

Exculpatory clause (exculpatory agreement)

purporting to excuse a party from liability resulting from negligence or an otherwise wrongful act

Noncompete agreement

an agreement btwn employer (principal) + employee (agent) to protect the employer's customers, trade secrets, confidential info, and other items for a specific period after termination

In pari delicto agreement

illegal transaction in which both parties are equally at fault

Severable contract

includes 2 or more promises, each of which a court can enforce separately

Review Questions

6-1. Explain why an insurance policy not covering an insurable interest is illegal and void.

they are considered wagering contracts because they gamble on others' lives or property

— increase the likelihood of intentional harm or destruction

6-2. Describe the recourse for an individual receiving services from an unlicensed professional.

the recipients of the services can refuse to pay for them because the contract was illegal

—trains, airplanes, buses, etc.

6-3. Explain why common carriers are generally restricted from limiting their liability for negligence unless permitted by statute, administrative agency ruling, or international agreement.

the lack of equality of bargaining power between large + powerful entities and the relatively powerless consumer is an important consideration when determining legal limits of liability

---

Educational Objective 7

Explain how each of the following may render a contract unenforceable:

- **Fraud**
- **Mistake**
- **Duress**
- **Undue influence**
- **Innocent misrepresentation**
- **Statute of frauds**
- **Parol evidence rule**

Key Words and Phrases

Genuine assent

contracting parties' actual assent to form a contract or their indication of intent to contract by their actions and words

Fraud

an intentional misrepresentation resulting in harm to a person or an organization

Representation

a statement of fact or opinion made by the insured when applying for insurance, usually in response to a question from the insurer

Material fact

in insurance, a fact that would affect the insurer's decision to provide or maintain insurance or to settle a claim

▶▶

Rescission

a legal action that voids a principal's bid
— plaintiff has no further duties under contract

Mistake

a perception that does not agree w/ the facts

Unilateral mistake

doesn't ordinarily affect contract

a perception by one party to a contract that does not agree w/ the facts

Bilateral mistake

generally makes contract voidable

a perception by both parties to a contract that does not agree w/ the facts

Duress

the use of restraint, violence, or threats of violence to compel a party to act contrary to his/her wishes or interests

Undue influence

the improper use of power or trust to deprive a person of free will and substitute another's objective, resulting in lack of genuine assent to a contract

Statute of frauds

a law to prevent fraud and perjury by requiring that certain contracts be in writing and contain the signature of the party responsible for performing that contract

Real property (realty)

tangible property consisting of land, all structures permanently attached to the land, and whatever is growing on the land

Uniform Commercial Code (UCC)

a model code that has been adopted in whole or in part by each state — its purpose is to provide a consistent legal basis for business transactions throughout the US and its territories

Condition precedent

an event that must occur before a duty of performance arises in a contract
i.e. delivery before performance

Review Questions

7-1. Describe the two remedies available to the plaintiff if fraud is proved in a given case.

7-2. Identify two requirements for an insurer to assert the concealment defense to an insurance contract.

7-3. Distinguish between unilateral and bilateral mistakes in a contract.

7-4. Explain why a person who has reasonably relied on an innocently misrepresented material fact can later avoid a contract.

7-5. Describe the purpose of the parol evidence rule.

Educational Objective 8
Paraphrase the rules on contract construction that courts commonly use to interpret contracts.

Key Word or Phrase

Parol evidence rule

a rule of evidence that limits the terms of a contract evidenced by a writing to those expressed in writing

Review Questions

8-1. Explain how courts apply established maxims of construction to interpret ambiguous contract language.

8-2. Contrast entire contracts with divisible contracts.

8-3. Explain why courts prefer to interpret contracts as divisible.

8-4. Describe the system of priorities courts apply to resolve contradictory contract terms.

Educational Objective 9
Describe the circumstances in which a third party would have enforceable rights under a contract.

Key Words and Phrases

Assignment

the transfer of rights or property

Assignor

the party to a contract who makes an assignment

Assignee

the individual or entity to whom property, rights, or interests have been transferred

Third-party beneficiary contract

a contract between two parties that benefits a 3rd party

Creditor beneficiary

a 3rd party beneficiary owed a debt that is to be satisfied by performance of a contract

Donee beneficiary

a 3rd party beneficiary who receives the benefit of a contract's performance as a gift from the promisee, w/ the intent of the contracting parties

Incidental beneficiary

a 3rd party beneficiary who has no contractual rights but benefits from a contract even though that is not the intent of the parties to the contract

Review Questions

9-1. List the most common situations in which contract rights are not assignable.

9-2. Describe an assignee's right under a contractual assignment.

9-3. Explain why the legal distinction between creditor and donee beneficiary contracts is becoming less important.

Educational Objective 10
Describe the various ways in which the contractual obligations of the parties to a contract can be terminated.

Key Words and Phrases

Tender

an offer to perform one's duties under a contract

Novation

Condition concurrent

Condition subsequent

Review Questions

10-1.   Explain how contracts promising or guaranteeing satisfaction are discharged.

10-2.   Describe the elements required for a novation to be effective.

10-3. Distinguish between frustration and impracticability as related to contract performance.

10-4. Identify four circumstances that may make performance of a contract impossible.

Educational Objective 11

Describe breach of contract in terms of the following:

- **Types of breach**
- **Remedies for breach**

Key Words and Phrases

Repudiation

Anticipatory breach

Material breach of contract

Compensatory damages

Consequential damages

Punitive damages (exemplary damages)

Bad faith (outrage)

Extracontractual damages

Mitigation of damages

Liquidated damages

Specific performance

Injunction

Review Questions

11-1. Compare material breaches of contract with minor breaches of contract.

11-2. Contrast compensatory damages and punitive damages in breach of contract lawsuits.

11-3. Explain when courts would order the equitable remedy of specific performance.

Educational Objective 12
Given a case, determine whether a described contract would be legally enforceable.

Application Question

12-1. Louis has been in negotiations to purchase Ed's yacht. Based on these negotiations, a price of $750,000 is established. Ed's attorney prepares the agreement indicating that the yacht will be conveyed at the stated price within sixty days.

    a. Have Louis and Ed formed a contract?

b.   At the closing, Louis inquires about the fishing gear and a large plasma
     television in the main cabin. Ed responds that these items are not included
     in the sale. Louis produces a letter from Ed dated one month prior to the
     agreement stating that all fishing gear is included in the sale of the yacht.
     Louis also maintains that Ed orally agreed to leave the plasma TV, as it
     would be very difficult to move. How do the statute of frauds and the parol
     evidence rule apply to this situation?

c.   Describe the five factors that would need to be proven to establish that
     Louis did not give genuine assent to the contract and to determine the
     enforceability of this agreement.

Answers to Assignment 2 Questions

NOTE: These answers are provided to give students a basic understanding of acceptable types of responses. They often are not the only valid answers and are not intended to provide an exhaustive response to the questions.

Educational Objective 1

1-1.   A bilateral contract is one in which each party becomes both a promisor and a promisee. If a default occurs, either party may enforce the other's promise in a legal action. In a unilateral contract, performance is required in exchange for the promise. A contract is not formed until performance occurs.

1-2.   A voidable contract is a valid contract that can continue in force unless an innocent party (such as a minor) chooses to avoid it, one of the contracting parties commits fraud, or the contract is found to be the result of duress on one of the parties. A void contract is an agreement that is not really a contract because it is not legally enforceable, such as an agreement to commit a crime.

Educational Objective 2

2-1.   The first requirement is the intent to contract. The offeror must intend, or appear to intend, to create a legally enforceable contract if the offeree accepts the offer. The second requirement of an offer is definite terms. The third requirement is communication to the offeree.

2-2.   Offers do not remain open indefinitely. An offer ceases to be binding when the time period the offer specifies expires or, absent a specific time period, when a reasonable amount of time passes. What is reasonable depends on considerations such as the contract's subject matter and the general commercial setting.

2-3.   Generally, an offeror can revoke, or withdraw, an offer any time before acceptance. As in the case of the offer itself, the revocation is effective only when communicated. The revocation must be communicated to the offeree and is effective only when the offeree actually receives it.

Educational Objective 3

3-1.   These answers refer to who can accept each specified type of offer:

   a.   An offer made to one person can only be accepted by the person to whom the offer is made, who is the offeree.

   b.   Any member of the group that has received the offer can accept it.

   c.   Anyone can accept an offer made to the public.

3-2.   Acceptance of an offer must be unconditional and unequivocal. If there is an acceptance that deviates from the offer's terms, it is a counteroffer.

3-3.   In a unilateral contract, performance of the contract is both acceptance and performance. Usually no communication other than performance or forbearance is required. In a bilateral contract, the offeree is typically required to communicate acceptance to the offeror.

Educational Objective 4

4-1. For an agreement to qualify as a contract, the parties to it must have legal capacity to contract. Capacity refers to one's ability to sue or be sued or to enter into an enforceable contract. Capacity includes the ability to understand the consequences of one's actions. A party deemed competent to contract is one who has the mental ability to understand problems and make decisions.

4-2. The four parties who typically lack capacity to contract are minors, insane persons, intoxicated persons (under the influence of alcohol or drugs), and artificial entities (such as insurers) that are restricted by law or corporate charter from entering into certain contracts.

4-3. Corporations, although artificial creations of the state, are persons in the eyes of the law. They can enter into contracts, and most states do not restrict the types of contracts they can make. However, the extent of the competence of a corporation to enter into a contract may be restricted by its corporate charter or, in the case of insurance, banking, and transportation corporations, by license or regulation.

Educational Objective 5

5-1. Valuable consideration is a legal benefit received by the promisor, such as money. Forbearance can be sufficient consideration to support a contract, such as a promise to refrain from an activity. Present consideration and future consideration, in contrast to past consideration, are both sufficient types of consideration to form an enforceable contract. Binding promises can also be sufficient consideration for forming an enforceable contract.

5-2. Past consideration is insufficient to support a contract. A promise to pay for performance previously completed without an agreement does not form an enforceable contract. A promise to perform an existing obligation, such as an obligation someone is legally required to perform, is also insufficient to form a binding contract. A compromise and release of claims does not form a binding contract, although there are exceptions.

5-3. Some contracts are enforceable despite a lack of consideration for equitable or public policy reasons or because state laws make specific exceptions. One example is promissory estoppel that applies when a party relies on the promise of the other party and only enforcement of the promise would achieve justice. Another example is a pledge made to a charitable organization.

5-4. There are several aspects of a property-casualty insurance contract:

   a. The insurer's consideration is its promise to indemnify, or pay on behalf of, an insured resulting from a covered occurrence.

   b. The insured's consideration is the premium payment or the promise of premium payment.

   c. Payment of the premium does not become an obligation until coverage begins.

Educational Objective 6

6-1. Such policies are considered wagering contracts because they gamble on others' lives or property and increase the likelihood of intentional harm or destruction.

6-2. If a person engages in an occupation without a required license, the recipients of that person's services can refuse to pay for them because the contract was illegal.

6-3. Common carriers are restricted due to the lack of equality of bargaining power between a large and powerful entity and the relatively powerless consumer.

Educational Objective 7

7-1. If fraud is proved, the plaintiff can seek one of two remedies:

- The plaintiff may seek rescission. If the court rescinds the contract, the plaintiff has no further duties under it and is entitled to reimbursement of all payments made to the defendant.

- If rescission would not make the plaintiff whole, the plaintiff can sue for damages in a tort action, usually called an action in deceit.

7-2. To assert the concealment defense, the insurer must prove two things:

- The insured knew that the fact concealed was material.

- The insured concealed the fact with the intent to defraud.

7-3. A unilateral mistake ordinarily does not affect a contract. Bilateral mistakes occur when both parties to a contract make the same mistake of fact. Under these conditions, contracts are generally voidable.

7-4. A person who has reasonably relied on an innocently misrepresented material fact can later avoid a resulting contract because of lack of genuine assent.

7-5. The parol evidence rule serves three purposes:

- To carry out the parties' presumed intention

- To achieve certainty and finality as to the parties' rights and duties

- To exclude fraudulent and perjured claims

Educational Objective 8

8-1. Maxims of construction are not strict legal rules but well-accepted guidelines for interpretation. They do not make a new contract or rewrite an old one. Courts apply them only to resolve doubts and ambiguities in a contract.

8-2. In an entire contract, one party must complete performance to be entitled to the other party's performance. In a divisible contract, the performance of a portion of the contract entitles the performing party to immediate payment.

8-3. Courts prefer to interpret contracts as divisible to avoid hardships that can result from delaying payments under the contract until full performance has been completed.

8-4. To resolve contradictory terms, courts apply this system of priorities:

- Handwriting prevails over typewriting.

- Typewriting prevails over printing.

- Words prevail over figures.

Educational Objective 9

9-1. Contract rights are not assignable in these situations:

- Laws restrict prior assignment of such rights as veterans' disability benefits, government pensions, wages, inheritances, and workers compensation benefits.

- The parties to an agreement might specify that they cannot, under the contract, assign the rights.

- Personal rights are not assignable.

- When an assignment materially alters or varies the obligor's performance, a court usually will not uphold it.

- When a judgment is pending in a personal injury case, generally the injured person cannot assign a claim for damages resulting from the injury.

9-2. As a general rule, the assignee's rights are those of the assignor and do not extend beyond them.

9-3. These two types of beneficiaries are often treated as one class, intended beneficiaries, who are third-party beneficiaries to whom a benefit was intended by the contracting parties.

Educational Objective 10

10-1. If a contract promises or guarantees satisfaction, unless the promisor can show bad faith on the promisee's part, obligations are not discharged until the promisee experiences personal and subjective satisfaction. Courts apply an objective standard to determine personal satisfaction relating to utility, fitness, or value.

10-2. For a novation to be effective, all parties must agree to the substitution. The remaining party must agree to accept the new party and must release the withdrawing party. The latter must consent to withdraw and to permit substitution of the new party. The presence of these essentials discharges the withdrawing party from the contract.

10-3. Frustration is the prevention of the attainment of a goal. To excuse a party's nonperformance of a contract, frustration must arise from an unforeseeable and uncontrollable circumstance that causes a fundamental change and that is the fault of neither party. Impracticability is an excuse for nonperformance of a contractual duty, the performance of which, though possible, would be extremely or unreasonably difficult.

10-4. These are four circumstances that may make performance of a contract impossible:

- If a change in law or a governmental act makes performance of an existing contract illegal, the promisor's performance is excused.

- The death or incapacitating illness of a specific person necessary to perform a personal service discharges the duty to perform.

- If the specific subject matter of the contract is destroyed or becomes nonexistent after contract formation without the promisor's fault, impossibility of performance discharges the promisor's duty.

- If the other party's act prevents the performance of a contract, a court will excuse performance.

Educational Objective 11

11-1.   The circumstances that affect the materiality of a breach include the extent to which the breaching party has performed, the willfulness of the breach, and the extent to which the nonbreaching party has obtained benefits and can receive adequate compensation. A material breach by one party excuses the other party's performance and immediately gives rise to remedies for breach of contract. A minor breach may temporarily suspend any duty of performance by the nonbreaching party or may give the aggrieved party a basis to sue for damages resulting from the breach, but not for breach of the entire contract.

11-2.   Compensatory damages are intended to place the injured party in approximately the position he or she would be in if the breaching party had performed the contract. Compensatory damages comprise the difference between the value of the promised performance and the plaintiff's cost of obtaining that performance elsewhere. They include losses caused by the breach and gains the breach prevented. Compensatory damages are typically awarded if a plaintiff prevails in a contract case. Punitive damages punish a defendant for a reckless, malicious, or deceitful act. Punitive damages are not usually appropriate in contract cases. If a seller of personal property commits fraud or misrepresentation, punitive damages can be appropriate; however, the punitive damages are usually based on the fraud, not on the breach of contract.

11-3.   Courts order the equitable remedy of specific performance when money damages would be inappropriate or inadequate. To determine whether money damages would be adequate, courts consider the difficulty of valuing the subject matter of the contract, the existence of unique qualities of the subject, and the difficulty or impossibility of obtaining a duplicate or substantial equivalent of the subject of the contract.

Educational Objective 12

12-1.   Answers are based on the facts presented in Louis' case.

   a.   Establishing a contract requires agreement, which consists of a valid offer and a valid acceptance. A valid offer requires three elements: intent to contract, definite terms, and communication to the other party. It appears that Louis had intent to contract for the purchase of this yacht. The agreement included definite terms identifying the parties, the subject matter, the price, and a time of performance. Louis signed and returned the agreement, thereby communicating to Ed and his attorney.

   b.   Most statutes of frauds and the Uniform Commercial Code (UCC) require that contracts related to the sale of goods in excess of $500 must be in writing. The parol evidence rule is based on the assumption that all prior negotiations, conversations, and agreements were merged into the final, written contract, which then becomes the complete statement of the parties' agreement. While it does not, on its own, make contracts unenforceable, it has important implications for contract interpretation, because once the parties have reduced any agreement to writing, no oral evidence may be admitted to contradict its terms. If the letter and conversation were not included in the final agreement, these items cannot alter the written agreement and any information contained in them are not enforceable at the time of closing.

   c.   Louis would have to prove that the contract was the result of fraud, that there was a mistake in the contract, or that he entered into the contract under duress. Additional factors include undue influence or reliance on an innocently misrepresented material fact.

Direct Your Learning

Contract Law: Insurance Applications

Educational Objectives

After learning the content of this assignment, you should be able to:

1. Describe these characteristics of insurance contracts:
   - A conditional contract
   - A contract involving fortuitous events and the exchange of unequal amounts
   - A contract of utmost good faith
   - A contract of adhesion
   - A contract of indemnity
   - A nontransferable contract

2. Describe the unique characteristics of insurance contract formation with regard to these aspects:
   - Agreement
   - Content
   - Delivery

3. Describe under what circumstances a third party can benefit from an insurance contract.

4. Explain how representations and warranties affect the creation and void-ability of an insurance contract.

5. Explain how the following concepts legally prevent an insurer from reviving a defense it has forfeited earlier:
   - Waiver
   - Estoppel
   - Election

3

Educational Objectives, continued

6. Explain how nonwaiver agreements and reservation of rights letters affect insurers' and insureds' rights.

Outline

▶ **Special Characteristics of Insurance Contracts**
  A. Conditional Contract
  B. Contract Involving Fortuitous Events and the Exchange of Unequal Amounts
  C. Contract of Utmost Good Faith
  D. Contract of Adhesion
  E. Contract of Indemnity
  F. Nontransferable Contract

▶ **Insurance Contract Formation**
  A. Agreement
    1. Offer and Acceptance
    2. Effective Date
    3. Silence or Delay
  B. Insurance Policy Content
    1. Written Versus Oral and Informal Written Contracts
    2. Necessary Terms in Insurance Contracts
    3. Implied Terms in Insurance Contracts
    4. Insurance Company Designation
  C. Delivery of Insurance Policies

▶ **Insurance as Third-Party Beneficiary Contract**
  A. Third-Party Interests in Liability Insurance
  B. Real Estate Sellers and Buyers
  C. Mortgagor's and Mortgagee's Interests
  D. Limited Interests in Realty
    1. Lease Interests
    2. Life Estates

▶ **Representations and Warranties in Insurance**
  A. Representations
    1. Elements Required to Establish False Representation
    2. Statutory Approaches to Misrepresentation
    3. Construction of Representations
  B. Warranties
    1. Warranties Distinguished From Representation
    2. Classification
    3. Lessening Warranty Effects

▶ **Waiver, Estoppel, and Election**
  A. Waiver
    1. Use of Waivers
    2. Consideration
    3. Knowledge Requirement
    4. Policy Provisions
    5. Acts Constituting Waiver
    6. Parol Evidence Rule
  B. Estoppel
    1. Insurance Law and Estoppel
    2. Distinguishing Estoppel From Waiver
    3. Factors Establishing Estoppel
  C. Election
    1. Application
    2. Insured's Election

▶ **Nonwaiver Agreements and Reservation of Rights Letters**
  A. Use of Nonwaiver Agreements and Reservation of Rights Letters
  B. Nonwaiver Agreements
  C. Reservation of Rights Letters
  D. Requirements for Nonwaiver Agreements and Reservation of Rights Letters

 **s.m.a.r.t. tips**   Use the SMART Online Practice Exams to test your understanding of the course material. You can review questions over a single assignment or multiple assignments, or you can take an exam over the entire course.

For each assignment, you should define or describe each of the Key Words and Phrases and answer each of the Review and Application Questions.

Educational Objective 1

Describe these characteristics of insurance contracts:

- **A conditional contract**
- **A contract involving fortuitous events and the exchange of unequal amounts**
- **A contract of utmost good faith**
- **A contract of adhesion**
- **A contract of indemnity**
- **A nontransferable contract**

Key Words and Phrases

Conditional contract

Utmost good faith

Misrepresentation

Incontestable clause

Contestable period

Contract of adhesion

Contract of indemnity

Principle of indemnity

Valued policy

Review Questions

1-1. Explain why insurance contracts are considered to involve an exchange of unequal amounts.

1-2. Identify the two things courts have held that insurers must prove to establish concealment of a material fact.

1-3. Contrast how the term "misrepresentation" is normally used with how the term is used with reference to insurance contracts.

1-4. Explain why insurance policies are nontransferable contracts.

Educational Objective 2

Describe the unique characteristics of insurance contract formation with regard to these aspects:

- **Agreement**
- **Content**
- **Delivery**

Key Word or Phrase

Binder

Review Questions

2-1. Describe the offer and acceptance components of an insurance contract.

2-2. Describe the circumstances under which an issued insurance policy might be an offer and not an acceptance of the contract.

2-3. Explain why courts have ruled that an insurer can be held liable under its contract if it delays action on an application beyond a reasonable time.

2-4. List the facts a court will consider when determining whether an insurer's response to an insurance application was unreasonably delayed.

2-5. Explain why written insurance policies are preferable to oral insurance contracts.

2-6. Explain why delivery of a contract is rarely in dispute in property-casualty insurance.

Educational Objective 3
Describe under what circumstances a third party can benefit from an insurance contract.

Key Word or Phrase

Direct-action statute

Review Questions

3-1. Explain why claimants under liability policies are not considered third-party beneficiaries in states that have not adopted direct-action statutes.

3-2. Explain why a buyer of real estate under an incomplete agreement of sale requires insurance on the property being sold.

3-3. Describe the situations that can occur when a mortgage does not specify who will obtain insurance on the property.

3-4. Describe the insurance protection available to cover a lessee's liability for caus-ing fire damage to a lessor's property.

Educational Objective 4

Explain how representations and warranties affect the creation and voidability of an insurance contract.

Review Questions

4-1. Describe the effect of a policyholder's false representation or misrepresentation of facts on an insurance application.

4-2. List the elements required for a plaintiff insurer to establish false representa-tion.

4-3. Explain why contribute-to-loss statutes create a more difficult standard for an insurer to show materiality sufficient to avoid a contract than do increase-of-risk statutes.

4-4. Describe the two requirements that must be present in order for a promise to be a warranty.

4-5. Contrast an affirmative warranty with a continuing (promissory) warranty.

4-6. Describe the effect on coverage when courts interpret policies as severable.

Educational Objective 5

Explain how the following concepts legally prevent an insurer from reviving a defense it has forfeited earlier:

- **Waiver**
- **Estoppel**
- **Election**

Key Words and Phrases

Waiver

Estoppel

Election

Review Questions

5-1. Describe the conditions required for a waiver of provisions under an insurance contract.

5-2. Explain why waivers are subject to the parol evidence rule.

5-3. Describe the sequence of events leading to estoppel in insurance law.

5-4. Distinguish waiver from estoppel.

Educational Objective 6
Explain how nonwaiver agreements and reservation of rights letters affect insurers' and insureds' rights.

Key Words and Phrases

Nonwaiver agreement

Reservation of rights letter

Review Questions

6-1. Explain how insurers use nonwaiver agreements and reservation of rights letters.

6-2. Describe the difficulties that may arise in securing an insured's consent and signature on a nonwaiver agreement.

6-3. Contrast a reservation of rights letter with a nonwaiver agreement.

Answers to Assignment 3 Questions

NOTE: These answers are provided to give students a basic understanding of acceptable types of responses. They often are not the only valid answers and are not intended to provide an exhaustive response to the questions.

Educational Objective 1

1-1. Insurance contracts involve an exchange of unequal amounts because often there are few or no losses, and the premium paid by the insured for a particular policy is more than the amount paid by the insurer to, or on behalf of, the insured. If a large loss occurs, however, the insurer's claim payment might be much more than the premium paid by the insured. The possibility that the insurer's obligation may be much greater than the insured's makes the insurance transaction a fair trade.

1-2. Courts have held that an insurer must prove these two things:

- The failure to disclose information was intentional, which is often difficult to establish.

- The information withheld was a material fact.

1-3. In normal usage, a misrepresentation is a false statement. As used in insurance, a misrepresentation is a false statement of a material fact on which the insurer relies.

1-4. The identities of the persons or organizations insured are extremely relevant to the insurer, which has the right to select those applicants with whom it is willing to enter into contractual agreements. After an insurance policy is in effect, an insured may not freely transfer, or assign, the policy to some other party.

Educational Objective 2

2-1. The insurance application, signed by the applicant and sent to the insurer through the producer, is the offer. The insurance policy issued later is the acceptance.

2-2. If the policy issued does not conform to the application—the initial offer—the policy is a counter-offer requiring the applicant's specific acceptance.

2-3. Courts apply the rationale in this situation that insurance is a business affected with a public interest. Because insurers have generally solicited these offers, and because applicants frequently pay premiums in advance, the insurer must act promptly in accepting or rejecting the offer.

2-4. A court will consider these facts regarding unreasonable delay:

- The distance of the insurer's office from the agent's office at which the applicant submitted the application

- Special difficulties in underwriting the risk

- The insurer's seasonal or other workload problems

- The type of coverage involved

2-5. Oral agreements often give rise to lawsuits, usually involving the insurer's word against the insured's, with a court making final judgment. An insured who does not have a written policy may be unable to recall an oral conversation with sufficient accuracy to persuade a jury of its content.

2-6. Delivery of a contract is rarely in dispute for property-casualty policies because of the wide use of preliminary oral agreements and written binders, which give rise to effective dates of coverage that seldom involve the question of policy delivery.

Educational Objective 3

3-1. In jurisdictions that have not adopted direct-action statues, the purpose of liability insurance is to indemnify only insureds for their losses in paying damages to the victims. In these situations, the third-party victims cannot sue under the liability policies until courts have ordered judgments against the insureds. If an insurer denies claim payments after a judgment, then a third party can sue an insurer directly.

3-2. A real estate buyer obtains an equitable interest in the property as soon as both parties sign the agreement of sale. The real estate belongs to the buyer, subject to the payment of the purchase price, under the doctrine of equitable conversion. One result of this equitable ownership is that the buyer bears the risk of loss and would therefore require an insurance policy to protect his or her interest in the property.

3-3. If the mortgage does not specify who will obtain insurance, one of three situations can occur:

- The mortgagor can obtain separate insurance on the property solely for the mortgagor's benefit.

- The mortgagee can obtain separate insurance on the property. If so, money the insurer pays in the event of loss does not accrue to the mortgagor's benefit and therefore is not payable to the mortgagor.

- The mortgagor can obtain insurance for the mortgagee's benefit by either assigning the policy to the mortgagee or including on the policy a standard mortgage clause making any proceeds under the policy payable to the mortgagee "as the mortgagee's interest may appear."

3-4. Insurance protection to cover a lessee's liability for fire damage to insured property can now take several forms:

- The insurer waives its subrogation rights against the lessee by endorsement to the lessor's fire policy.

- A lease provision placing "all-risks" loss on the lessor is included on the policy.

- The lessee is included as an additional insured on the lessor's policy.

- The lessee purchases an insurance policy protecting against liability for causing damage to the lessor's property.

- The lessee purchases a separate fire policy covering the leased premises.

Educational Objective 4

4-1. False representation, or misrepresentation, may make an insurance contract voidable.

4-2. These are the elements required to establish false representation:

- A statement is made that is false or misleading.

- The statement relates to a material fact.

- The insurer relies on the false or misleading statement in issuing the policy.

4-3. The rule under most contribute-to-loss statutes is that, regardless of materiality, a misrepresentation does not allow an insurer to avoid the contract if, from its very nature, it could not contribute to the loss. Increase-of-risk statutes can set either an objective or a subjective standard for determining materiality.

4-4. These two requirements must be present for a promise to be a warranty:

- The parties must have clearly and unmistakably intended it to be a warranty.

- The statement must form a part of the contract itself.

4-5. An affirmative warranty states that specific facts exist at the time the contract forms. A continuing, or promissory, warranty states that the parties will do certain things or that certain conditions will continue to exist during the policy term.

4-6. When courts interpret policies as severable, if one policy provision is invalid, it need not invalidate the entire policy but can be severed, or separated, from other provisions. Therefore, noncompliance with a warranty concerning one type of covered property will not defeat coverage for another type of property to which the warranty does not relate.

Educational Objective 5

5-1. For waiver to occur, an insurance policy must exist. A statement made before an insurance contract comes into existence is not a waiver of a known right, but an attempted waiver of a future right.

5-2. The parol evidence rule prohibits the introduction into evidence at trial of any oral agreements made before, or contemporaneous with, the formation of a written contract. The law assumes that final written insurance policies contain all waiver agreements that have arisen from words or acts before or during the writing of the policy.

5-3. Estoppel arises in insurance law from this sequence of events:

- False representation of a material fact

- Reasonable reliance on the representation

- Resulting injury or detriment to the insured

5-4. Waiver differs from estoppel in these ways:

- Waiver is contractual and rests upon agreement between parties. Estoppel is equitable and arises from false representation.

- Waiver gives effect to the waiving party's intention. Estoppel defeats the inequitable intent of the estopped party.

- The parol evidence rule applies to waiver but not to estoppel.

Educational Objective 6

6-1. Insurers use nonwaiver agreements and reservation of rights letters to inform an insured that the insurer's activities regarding a loss are not the relinquishment of its right to stand on policy provisions. An insurer might be able to establish that it is not liable under the policy. The insurer can continue to investigate and evaluate the loss on its merits, an activity beneficial to both the insurer's and insured's interests. Simultaneously, the insurer can determine whether the insured has violated policy terms and whether the insurer will accept liability under the policy.

6-2. These practical difficulties may arise in the attempt to secure the insured's consent and signature on a nonwaiver agreement:

- The insured might refuse to sign the agreement, even after the claims representative has clearly explained its significance. This refusal can delay the investigation of the loss.

- The insured could challenge the nonwaiver agreement if the claims representative has not explained the importance of the agreement fully and fairly. The lack of adequate explanation can lead an insured to claim lack of contractual intent, misunderstanding, duress, or other defenses that can jeopardize the agreement's validity.

6-3. A reservation of rights letter serves the same purpose as a nonwaiver agreement but is in letter form, and it is a unilateral document, meaning it does not require the insured to sign or agree to the contents of the letter.

Direct Your Learning

Commercial Law

Educational Objectives

After learning the content of this assignment, you should be able to:

1. Summarize the significance of each of the following in relation to the creation and performance of a contract for the sale of goods:

    - Uniform Commercial Code Article 2

    - Types of sales contracts

    - Formation of sales contracts

    - Breach of sales contracts and remedies for the breach

2. Summarize the significance of each of the following in the sale of goods that occurs at a distance or over time:

    - Uniform Commercial Code Article 3

    - Types of commercial paper

    - Transfer and negotiation

    - Holders in due course

3. Describe the creation and uses of the following:

    - Warehouse receipt

    - Bill of lading

4. Explain the following aspects of secured transactions in (or for) the sale of goods:

    - Uses of security interests

    - Forms of security interests

    - Attachment of security interests

    - Perfection of security interests

    - Rights of perfected and unperfected security interests

    - Default

4

5. Explain how each of the following helps to ensure fair treatment of consumers in dealings with suppliers of goods and services:

    - Fair trade laws

    - Consumer credit laws

    - Bankruptcy

Outline

▶ **Sales Contracts**
  A. UCC Article 2
  B. Types of Sales Contracts
  C. Formation of Sales Contracts
    1. Offer
    2. Acceptance
    3. Consideration
    4. Statute of Frauds
  D. Performance
    1. Title and Risk of Loss
    2. Delivery Terms
    3. Inspection
    4. Time for Delivery
    5. Conforming and Nonconforming Goods
    6. Express and Implied Warranties
  E. Breach of Sales Contracts and Remedies
    1. Revocation of Acceptance
    2. Excuses for Nonperformance
    3. Seller's Remedies
    4. Buyer's Remedies
▶ **Negotiable Instruments**
  A. UCC Article 3
  B. Types of Commercial Paper
  C. Transfer and Negotiation
    1. Primary and Secondary Liability
    2. Endorsements
  D. Holders in Due Course
▶ **Documents of Title**
  A. UCC Article 7
  B. Documents of Title
    1. Warehouse Receipt
    2. Bill of Lading
    3. Delivery Order
▶ **Secured Transactions**
  A. UCC Article 9
  B. Forms of Secured Transactions
  C. Forms of Collateral
  D. Attachment

  E. Perfecting a Security Interest
  F. Rights of Perfected and Unperfected Security Interests
  G. Satisfaction of a Secured Debt
  H. Default
▶ **Consumer Protection Laws**
  A. Fair Trade Laws
    1. Federal Trade Commission Act
    2. State Unfair Trade Practices Acts
    3. Magnuson-Moss Warranty Act
  B. Consumer Credit Laws
    1. Truth in Lending Act
    2. Electronic Fund Transfer Act
    3. Fair Credit Reporting Act
    4. Equal Credit Opportunity Act
  C. Bankruptcy
    1. Federal Bankruptcy Act
    2. Liquidation Proceedings

 **s.m.a.r.t. tips** The SMART Online Practice Exams can be tailored to cover specific assignments, so you can focus your studies on topics you want to master.

For each assignment, you should define or describe each of the Key Words and Phrases and answer each of the Review and Application Questions.

Educational Objective 1

Summarize the significance of each of the following in relation to the creation and performance of a contract for the sale of goods:

- **Uniform Commercial Code Article 2**
- **Types of sales contracts**
- **Formation of sales contracts**
- **Breach of sales contracts and remedies for the breach**

Key Words and Phrases

Statutes of fraud

Risk

COD (collect on delivery)

Implied warranty of merchantability

Implied warranty of fitness for a particular purpose

Implied warranty of title

Review Questions

1-1. Identify the type of transactions for which the Uniform Commercial Code (UCC) Article 2 applies.

1-2. Contrast unilateral contracts with bilateral contracts.

1-3. Describe the two situations under which an oral contract for the sale of goods for $500 or more is enforceable.

1-4. Compare the costs paid by a seller with cost-insurance-freight (CIF) delivery terms to those paid in a free on board (FOB) place of shipment sale.

1-5. Describe the two exceptions to the rule that a shipment of nonconforming goods constitutes a breach of contract.

1-6. Describe the remedy for a seller that discovers the buyer is insolvent once the goods are en route.

Educational Objective 2

Summarize the significance of each of the following in the sale of goods that occurs at a distance or over time:

- **Uniform Commercial Code Article 3**
- **Types of commercial paper**
- **Transfer and negotiation**
- **Holders in due course**

Key Words and Phrases

Uniform Commercial Code (UCC)

Primary liability

Secondary liability

Personal defense

Real defense

Review Questions

2-1. Describe the Uniform Commercial Code (UCC) requirements for an instrument to be negotiable.

2-2. Why is salability an essential characteristic for negotiable instruments?

2-3. How can the payee of a negotiable instrument negotiate it to another specific person?

2-4. Describe a holder in due course.

Application Question

2-5. Describe these endorsements found on separate instruments, on each of which John Doe is payee, and point out the liabilities, if any, incurred by John Doe:

   a. Pay to the order of Howard Roe /s/ John Doe

   b. For deposit /s/ John Doe

   c. Pay to the order of Susan Coe without recourse /s/ John Doe

Educational Objective 3

Describe the creation and uses of the following:

- **Warehouse receipt**
- **Bill of lading**

Key Words and Phrases

Warehouse receipt

Bill of lading

Carrier

Bailment

Bailor

Bailee

Consignor

Consignee

Review Questions

3-1. Describe what is defined as a document of title under UCC 1-201 (b) (16).

3-2. Identify the information included on a warehouse receipt.

3-3. List the purposes served by a bill of lading.

Educational Objective 4

Explain the following aspects of secured transactions in (or for) the sale of goods:

- **Uses of security interests**
- **Forms of security interests**
- **Attachment of security interests**
- **Perfection of security interests**
- **Rights of perfected and unperfected security interests**
- **Default**

Key Words and Phrases

Collateral

Security interest

Pledge

Chattel

Perfected security interest

Constructive notice

Holder in due course

Lien

Review Questions

4-1. Describe the chattel mortgage form of secured transactions.

4-2. Identify the five general forms of collateral.

4-3. Describe the three requirements for an attachment to occur as a security interest in property.

4-4. Explain why a debtor should request a termination statement once a secured debt has been repaid.

4-5. Describe how a creditor could use the right to regain possession to foreclose on an unpaid debt.

Educational Objective 5

Explain how each of the following helps to ensure fair treatment of consumers in dealings with suppliers of goods and services:

- **Fair trade laws**
- **Consumer credit laws**
- **Bankruptcy**

Key Word or Phrase

Bankruptcy law

Review Questions

5-1. Describe the Federal Trade Commission (FTC) Act.

    a.   Compare the FTC Act to the Sherman Anti-Trust Act.

    b.   Does the FTC Act apply to the insurance industry?

5-2. Describe practices typically prohibited by state unfair trade practices acts.

    a.   Compare state unfair trade practices acts with the FTC Act.

b.   Describe state unfair trade practices acts specific to insurance.

5-3. Compare the Magnuson-Moss Act with the Uniform Commercial Code (UCC) provisions relating to warranties.

a.   Compare provisions of the Magnuson-Moss Act with those of the UCC regarding implied warranties.

b.   Why do manufacturers characterize warranties as limited warranties when they are essentially full warranties?

5-4. Describe the purpose of the Truth in Lending Act.

a.   Describe the Fair Credit Billing Act, an amendment to the Truth in Lending Act.

b. Describe the Fair Debt Collection Practices Act, an amendment to the Truth in Lending Act.

5-5. Describe the two avenues of relief provided by bankruptcy law.

Application Question

5-6. John and Mary Doe apply for Chapter 7 bankruptcy relief and enter liquidation proceedings. What is the goal of their bankruptcy?

a. List the parties to the bankruptcy proceeding.

b. John is halfway through the process of repaying federally guaranteed student loans for his MBA program. Is it likely that those loans will be discharged in the bankruptcy?

Answers to Assignment 4 Questions

NOTE: These answers are provided to give students a basic understanding of acceptable types of responses. They often are not the only valid answers and are not intended to provide an exhaustive response to the questions.

Educational Objective 1

1-1. UCC Article 2 applies to commercial transactions such as the sale of goods, leases, contracts, and negotiable instruments.

1-2. Under a unilateral contract, a promise is exchanged for an act. A bilateral contract is an exchange of promises of future action.

1-3. The two situations in which an oral contract for the sale of goods for $500 or more is enforceable are these:

- The buyer accepts and receives part of the goods.

- The buyer makes partial or full payment for the goods.

1-4. A seller pays the cost of insurance and freight charges for delivery to the buyer in a CIF sale, but not in an FOB sale. In an FOB place of shipment sale, the seller delivers goods to the carrier at the seller's risk and expense, and the ownership then shifts to the buyer.

1-5. The two exceptions to the rule that a shipment of nonconforming goods constitutes a breach of contract are these:

- A shipment of nonconforming goods is neither an acceptance nor a breach of contract if the seller notifies the buyer that the shipment is only an accommodation to the buyer.

- If a buyer rejects goods as nonconforming, the seller can notify the buyer of its intention to "cure" the nonconformity of the shipment by delivering conforming goods.

1-6. If the goods are en route, the seller can stop delivery unless the buyer has already received a document of title for the goods or unless a carrier or warehouse operator has notified the buyer that it is holding the goods for the buyer.

Educational Objective 2

2-1. An instrument must be in writing and meet these four requirements to be negotiable:

- It must be signed by the maker or drawer.

- It must contain an unconditional promise or order to pay a certain sum of money and contain no other promise, order, obligation, or power on the part of the drawer or maker except as otherwise provided by Article 3.

- It must be payable on demand or at a definite time.

- It must be payable to order or to bearer.

2-2. Salability is an essential characteristic for negotiable instruments so that the seller does not have to wait for payment once the goods are delivered to the buyer.

2-3. The payee of a negotiable instrument can negotiate it to another specific person by endorsement.

2-4. A holder in due course is the person to whom a negotiable instrument has been issued or endorsed and who possesses it for value, in good faith, and without notice that it may not be valid, can be claimed by another, is overdue, or was previously dishonored.

2-5. The answers to the questions about the endorsements on separate instruments are these:

    a.   This is a special endorsement that transfers John Doe's right to payment associated with the check to Howard Roe. This endorsement, however, does not transfer John Doe's liabilities. If the check is dishonored, John Doe will have liability to Howard Roe for the payment.

    b.   This is a restrictive endorsement that limits payment of the check to a deposit into an account or fund owned by John Doe. John Doe retains liability to the financial institution holding the account if the check is dishonored.

    c.   This is a qualified endorsement that transfers John Doe's rights and liabilities to Susan Coe. John Doe is not liable to Susan Coe or any future holders if the check is dishonored.

Educational Objective 3

3-1. UCC 1-201 (b) (16) defines a document of title as a bill of lading, dock warrant, dock receipt, warehouse receipt, order for the delivery of goods, or any other document that, in the regular course of business or financing, adequately evidences that the possessor is entitled to receive, hold, and dispose of the document and the goods it covers.

3-2. Warehouse operators provide the goods' owner with a receipt describing the amount, type, and condition of the goods, and the conditions of storage.

3-3. The bill of lading serves these purposes:

- As a contract for the transportation (carriage) of the goods

- As a receipt of the goods by the carrier for delivery

- Under certain circumstances, as title to the goods

- To identify the terms of the agreement, including goods by type and amount, the consignor, the carrier, provisions of the agreement for shipping, any special instructions, the consignee, date shipped, terms of delivery, and freight terms (prepaid, collect, or from a third party).

Educational Objective 4

4-1. In a chattel mortgage, the debtor is allowed to retain possession of the property while the creditor retains the right to take ownership of the property.

4-2. Most collateral falls into one of five forms:

- Consumer goods

- Equipment

- Farm products

- Inventory

- Property on paper

4-3.   There are three requirements for an attachment to occur:

- A consensual security agreement must exist between the debtor and creditor.

- The creditor must give value.

- The debtor must have rights in the collateral.

4-4.   The debtor can send a written request to the creditor for a termination statement and then file a termination statement with all offices that hold the financing statement. A termination statement is evidence that the debt has been paid in full.

4-5.   The secured party has the right to regain possession of collateral through the courts or by other legal means, such as lawful repossession. The majority of states allow the secured party to regain possession without going to court if the collateral can be repossessed in a legal manner.

Educational Objective 5

5-1.   The FTC Act prohibits unfair methods of competition and unfair or deceptive acts or practices that affect interstate commerce.

a.   The FTC Act is not strictly an antitrust act, although it overlaps with the Sherman Anti-Trust Act. The purpose of the Sherman Anti-Trust Act was to prevent companies from acting in ways that would hinder free competition by outlawing practices such as unlawful restraints of trade, price discrimination, price fixing, and unlawful monopolies. The FTC Act is broader than the antitrust acts in that it prohibits unfair or deceptive acts that have no relationship to competition.

b.   The FTC Act does not apply to the insurance industry. Under the McCarran-Ferguson Act, the federal government generally does not regulate the business of insurance because it is subject to state regulation. However, if a state does not have antitrust legislation, federal antitrust laws apply. Even if states do regulate insurance antitrust matters, federal antitrust laws can apply in cases of insurance practices involving boycott, coercion, or intimidation.

5-2.   State laws typically prohibit unfair acts (oppressive or bad-faith conduct), deceptive acts (fraud, deceit, and misrepresentation), and unfair methods of competition (including antitrust violations such as price fixing and group boycotts).

a.   State laws are designed to compensate for perceived inadequacies in the FTC Act. For example, some states extend rights to sue that the FTC Act does not provide. Many of the state acts apply to insurance, unlike the FTC Act.

b.   State unfair trade practices acts and unfair claim settlement practices acts specific to insurance generally follow the National Association of Insurance Commissioners (NAIC) model Insurance Fair Trade Practices Act. State unfair trade practices acts prohibit such unfair and deceptive insurance industry practices as misrepresentation and false advertising of policies; defamation of competitors; boycott, coercion, and intimidation; creation of false financial statements; unfair discrimination; rebates; and issuing capital stock, certificates, or securities or using advisory board or similar contracts that promise returns or profits as an inducement to purchase insurance.

5-3.   The UCC codified implied warranties of merchantability and fitness for a particular purpose and described the creation of express warranties. However, under the UCC, only consumers could enforce these warranties, and consumers could also unwittingly waive them. Inadequate controls led to increasing deception in product warranties and resulted in the passage of the Magnuson-Moss Act. The Magnuson-Moss Act does not require a producer of goods to provide a warranty. However, if the producer does provide a written warranty, it must conform to certain standards. The FTC enforces Magnuson-Moss on the federal level.

   a.   The UCC provides for implied warranties of merchantability and fitness for a particular purpose but allows sellers to disclaim them. Magnuson-Moss does not permit disclaimers of implied warranties. Under a full warranty, implied warranties cannot be limited in any way. However, Magnuson-Moss does permit a limited warranty to apply the same time restriction to implied warranties as that specified in the express warranty.

   b.   Manufacturers often characterize warranties that are essentially full warranties as limited to avoid the "lemon law" provision of Magnuson-Moss that applies to full warranties. If repeated efforts to repair a product fail, lemon provisions require that consumers of such products must have a choice of full refund or a replacement without charge.

5-4.   The purpose of the Truth in Lending Act is to ensure that consumers know the terms and interest rates of their credit transactions.

   a.   Under the Fair Credit Billing Act, a person who is dissatisfied with property or services purchased with a credit card has the right not to pay the remaining amount due if he or she first tries in good faith to return the property or give the merchant a chance to correct the problem.

   b.   The Fair Debt Collection Practices Act prohibits unfair and oppressive collection practices by agencies that collect debt for creditors.

5-5.   Bankruptcy law provides two avenues for relief. One avenue is the liquidation of the debtor's assets and distribution of the proceeds to the creditors. The other avenue is a reorganization of the debtor's affairs, free of creditor's claims during the process, and partial or full repayment of their debts.

5-6.   The goal of John and Mary Doe's bankruptcy is to discharge all debts prior to the court's order for relief in order to give them a fresh start.

   a.   The parties to a federal bankruptcy proceeding include the debtor, the creditors (both secured and unsecured), a trustee, a bankruptcy judge, and attorneys.

   b.   Bankruptcy does not discharge all debts. Education loans are typically not discharged by bankruptcy.

Direct Your Learning

Property Law

Educational Objectives

After learning the content of this assignment, you should be able to:

1. Explain how a person can acquire ownership of personal property in each of these ways:

   - Creation

   - Accession

   - Confusion

   - Gifts

   - Bailments

2. Describe the respective rights and duties of a bailee and a bailor.

3. Describe these types of real property ownership:

   - Fee simple estate

   - Life estate

   - Joint tenancy

   - Tenancy by the entirety

   - Tenancy in common

   - Community property

   - Cooperative ownership

   - Condominium ownership

4. Describe real property sales in terms of the following:

   - The required elements of a contract of sale

   - The types of deeds and the characteristics of each

   - The requirements that deeds must meet

5

- How and why deeds are recorded

5. Describe the purpose and operation of each of the following:
   - Mortgages
   - Trust deeds
   - Land contracts
   - Mechanic's liens

6. Describe each of the following incidental real property rights:
   - Adverse possession
   - Rights to whatever is under, above, or on the land's surface
   - Rights to lateral and subjacent support
   - Water rights
   - Ownership of fixtures

7. Describe the following types of land use restrictions:
   - Incorporeal interests
   - Licenses
   - Government controls

8. Describe the landlord-tenant relationship in terms of the following:
   - The three types of landlord-tenant estates
   - Landlord's rights and duties
   - Landlord's remedies
   - Tenant's rights and duties

Outline

▶ **Ownership and Possession of Personal Property**
  A. Basic Concepts of Property Law
  B. Creation of Intellectual Property
    1. Copyrights
    2. Patents
  C. Accession
  D. Confusion
  E. Gifts
  F. Bailments
▶ **Bailee's and Bailor's Rights and Duties**
  A. Bailee's Rights
  B. Bailee's Duties
  C. Bailor's Rights and Duties
▶ **Real Property Ownership**
  A. Estate in Fee Simple
  B. Life Estate
  C. Concurrent Estates
    1. Joint Tenancy
    2. Tenancy by the Entirety
    3. Tenancy in Common
    4. Community Property
  D. Cooperative Ownership
  E. Condominium Ownership
▶ **Real Property Sales**
  A. Elements of a Contract of Sale
  B. Types of Deeds
  C. Requirements That Deeds Must Meet
  D. Recording Deeds
▶ **Real Property Security Interests and Liens**
  A. Mortgages
  B. Trust Deeds
  C. Land Contracts
  D. Mechanics' Liens on Real Property
    1. Priorities for Mechanics' Liens
    2. Waiver of Lien
▶ **Incidental Real Property Rights**
  A. Adverse Possession

  B. Rights Under, Above, and on the Land's Surface
  C. Rights to Lateral and Subjacent Support
  D. Water Rights
  E. Ownership of Fixtures
▶ **Land Use Restrictions**
  A. Incorporeal Interests
    1. Easements
    2. Profits à Prendre
    3. Seller's Restrictions on Land Use
  B. Licenses
  C. Government Controls
    1. Zoning
    2. Building Codes
    3. Eminent Domain
▶ **The Landlord and Tenant Relationship**
  A. Types of Landlord-Tenant Estates
  B. Landlord's Rights and Duties
  C. Landlord's Remedies
  D. Tenant's Rights and Duties

 When you take the randomized full practice exams in the SMART Online Practice Exams product, you are seeing the same kinds of questions you will see when you take the actual exam.

For each assignment, you should define or describe each of the Key Words and Phrases and answer each of the Review and Application Questions.

Educational Objective 1

Explain how a person can acquire ownership of personal property in each of these ways:

- **Creation**
- **Accession**
- **Confusion**
- **Gifts**
- **Bailments**

Key Words and Phrases

Intellectual property rights

Copyright

Patent

Accession

Confusion

Gift

Donee

Bailment

Review Questions

1-1. Distinguish between the rights of ownership and possession.

1-2. Describe the two categories of property.

1-3. Describe the factors courts consider when determining fair use of copyrighted material.

1-4. Describe the donative intent element of a gift.

Educational Objective 2
Describe the respective rights and duties of a bailee and a bailor.

Key Word or Phrase

Possessory lien

Review Questions

2-1. Describe the bailee's rights in a bailment for the bailor's sole benefit.

2-2. Describe the degree of care required in a bailment for the bailor's and bailee's mutual benefit.

2-3. Explain the extent of a bailee's insurable interest.

2-4. Define what is meant by negligent entrustment.

Educational Objective 3

Describe these types of real property ownership:

- **Fee simple estate**
- **Life estate**
- **Joint tenancy**
- **Tenancy by the entirety**
- **Tenancy in common**
- **Community property**
- **Cooperative ownership**
- **Condominium ownership**

Key Words and Phrases

Fee simple estate

Life estate

Tenancy

Joint tenancy

Tenancy by the entirety

Tenancy in common

Community property

Cooperative ownership

Condominium

Review Questions

3-1. Distinguish between joint tenancies and tenancies in common.

3-2. Explain how a tenancy by the entirety differs from a joint tenancy.

3-3. Describe the disadvantages of cooperative ownership.

3-4. Describe the two legal elements of condominium ownership.

Educational Objective 4

Describe real property sales in terms of the following:

- **The required elements of a contract of sale**
- **The types of deeds and the characteristics of each**
- **The requirements that deeds must meet**
- **How and why deeds are recorded**

Key Words and Phrases

Deed

Vendor

Vendee

Grantor

Grantee

Review Questions

4-1. Describe the two essential terms contained in a contract for the sale of real estate.

4-2. Contrast a general warranty deed with a special warranty deed.

4-3. Explain why it is important that a deed be absolutely accurate.

4-4. Describe the purpose of recording a deed.

Educational Objective 5

Describe the purpose and operation of each of the following:

- **Mortgages**
- **Trust deeds**
- **Land contracts**
- **Mechanic's liens**

Key Words and Phrases

Mortgagor

Mortgagee

Foreclosure

Trust deed (deed of trust or trust indenture)

Mechanic's lien

Review Questions

5-1. Identify the specific rights of a mortgagor.

5-2. Describe the mortgagee's remedy when the mortgagor fails to make payments on the mortgage and defaults.

5-3. List the three parties in a trust deed.

5-4. Explain how a land contract operates for these parties:

a. The buyer

b.   The seller

5-5.   List the facts that a general contractor must show when asserting a mechanic's lien against a customer's property.

Educational Objective 6

Describe each of the following incidental real property rights:

- **Adverse possession**
- **Rights to whatever is under, above, or on the land's surface**
- **Rights to lateral and subjacent support**
- **Water rights**
- **Ownership of fixtures**

Key Words and Phrases

Adverse possession

Lateral support

Subjacent support

Trade fixtures

Improvements and betterments

Review Questions

6-1. List the four elements required for one to obtain title by adverse possession of the lands of another.

6-2. Describe the limited rights a landowner has over the airspace above the land.

6-3. Describe the water rights of landowners with surface streams passing through the property.

6-4. Identify the tests for whether a particular property is a fixture.

Educational Objective 7
Describe the following types of land use restrictions:

- **Incorporeal interests**
- **Licenses**
- **Government controls**

Key Words and Phrases
Incorporeal interest

Easement

Profits à prendre

License

Zoning

Exclusionary zoning

Spot zoning

Special exception

Variance

Hardship variance

Use variance

Nonconforming use

Building codes

Eminent domain

Condemnation proceeding

Review Questions

7-1. Explain how easements are created.

7-2. Give examples of profits *à prendre*.

7-3. Contrast zoning laws and building codes with respect to the matters they typically control.

7-4. List the two conditions for granting a petition to seize property through eminent domain.

Application Question

7-5. In 2005, Bryan sold some land to Oliver. The deed provided that there could be no automobile garage on the premises and no building used for the manufacture of glue, gun powder, or fertilizers on the premises. Are the restrictions binding on Oliver? Explain.

Educational Objective 8

Describe the landlord-tenant relationship in terms of the following:

- **The three types of landlord-tenant estates**
- **Landlord's rights and duties**
- **Landlord's remedies**
- **Tenant's rights and duties**

Key Words and Phrases

Tenancy at will

Estate for years

Periodic tenancy

Holdover tenant

Review Questions

8-1. Describe the landlord's primary duty.

8-2. Summarize a landlord's remedies against a tenant when the tenant remains in possession at lease termination.

8-3. Describe a tenant's primary rights and duties.

8-4. Explain who is liable for injuries to third parties on rented or leased property.

Answers to Assignment 5 Questions

NOTE: These answers are provided to give students a basic understanding of acceptable types of responses. They often are not the only valid answers and are not intended to provide an exhaustive response to the questions.

Educational Objective 1

1-1. Ownership is a relationship between the owner and the rest of society that includes rights of the owner specific to the property. Possession is the exercise of custody or control over property and is not, in itself, ownership.

1-2. The two categories of property are real property and personal property. Real property is land including structures or rights attached to the land and the rights to water, minerals, and things attached to land, such as buildings, trees, and fixtures that have become part of the realty. Personal property is all property that is not real property.

1-3. Courts consider these factors in determining fair use:

- Purpose of the use

- Nature of the work

- Amount and substantiality of the portion used

- Effect of the use on the work's value

- Extent to which the use might deprive the copyright owner of economic advantage

1-4. The donor must intend to make a gift in the present. A promise to make a future gift is not enforceable.

Educational Objective 2

2-1. A bailee may use or handle the property only to the extent necessary to preserve and protect it.

2-2. When the bailment is for the bailor's and bailee's mutual benefit, the bailee must exercise reasonable care under the circumstances.

2-3. Because of the bailee's legal duty to care for the goods and to return them to the bailor, the bailee has an insurable interest in the goods and can obtain insurance to protect that interest.

2-4. Negligent entrustment is leaving a dangerous article, such as a gun or car, with a person who the lender knows, or should know, is likely to use it in an unreasonably risky manner.

Educational Objective 3

3-1. In joint tenancies, the estate goes entirely to the other joint tenant in the event of one joint tenant's death. Also, with two joint tenants, each must hold a one-half share. One of the joint tenants cannot be subject to a condition that does not apply to the others. The same deed must name them all as owners. Tenancies in common, however, involve no survivorship, allow parties to own unequal shares, and do not require parties to derive their interests in the same deed from the same grantor.

3-2. A tenancy by the entirety involves a husband and wife and differs from a joint tenancy because a sale or contract to sell does not sever the tenancy, and individual creditors of either the husband or the wife cannot subject the property to a claim. Also, unless both spouses are found liable for the same tort, judgment creditors cannot execute on the marital property. Finally, neither party individually owns a portion that can be mortgaged.

3-3. One disadvantage is the owner's limited control over external conditions, which can lead to a deterioration of the investment. Finding a purchaser for the premises can be difficult, particularly if it is beginning to deteriorate. Additionally, if other tenants do not keep up their payments, and as a result the mortgage payments lapse, the mortgagee can foreclose on the property. In that case, all tenants can lose any equity they have built up in the property.

3-4. The two legal elements of condominium ownership are individual ownership of a unit, or separate, defined area, and an undivided interest in common or public areas that serve all individual units.

Educational Objective 4

4-1. The contract must describe the premises to be sold and the price.

4-2. A general warranty deed, in addition to transferring whatever title the grantor has, contains the grantor's warranty that the title is free of all encumbrances, that the grantor has the title being transferred, and that no one else has a better title. A special warranty deed contains warranties against only those encumbrances and defects in the title that might have been created since the grantor took title.

4-3. A deed must be absolutely accurate—more so than the contract of sale because if the two conflict, the deed prevails.

4-4. The purpose of recording is to give notice to the world that the transfer of real property has occurred.

Educational Objective 5

5-1. The mortgagor has the specific rights to sell, lease, or even put another mortgage on property.

5-2. Mortgage foreclosure is the mortgagee's remedy when the mortgagor defaults on mortgage payments. Foreclosure through public sale is the most common method.

5-3. A trust deed has three parties: (1) the borrower (trustor) who transfers the land; (2) the trustee, to whom the land is transferred; and (3) the beneficiaries, for whose benefit the transfer is made.

5-4. This is how a contract of land operates for these parties:

   a. The buyer takes possession of the land, pays all the taxes and assessments, insures the property, repairs it, and assumes all the obligations of an owner.

   b. The seller has only the legal title; however, if the buyer defaults, the seller can declare the contract breached and repossess the property, treating the buyer as an ordinary tenant.

5-5. The general contractor must show these facts:

- Substantial performance of the contract

- Improvement of a specific piece of property under the contract

- Specific mention in the contract of the property to be improved

Educational Objective 6

6-1. The elements required for obtaining title by adverse possession of another person's land are these:

- The adverse party must have exclusive possession of the property and occupy it in the usual way.

- Possession must be open and obvious.

- Possession must be adverse, or hostile, and without the owner's permission.

- Possession must be continuous for a statutory period, usually a lengthy period, such as twenty years or more.

6-2. A landowner can halt unauthorized intrusion into the airspace over their land, such as projections from an adjoining building or utility lines stretched across the airspace. Generally, planes can fly over land as long as they do not interfere unreasonably with the owner's use and enjoyment of the land.

6-3. Owners of property that has surface streams passing through can use as much water from the waterway as needed for domestic purposes but must use only a reasonable amount for industrial purposes and must consider downstream owners' needs.

6-4. Three tests determine whether property is a fixture:

a. The article cannot be removed without substantial injury to the realty.

b. The article is specially constructed or fitted for use in a building, or the article is installed in the building to enable people to use the building.

c. The party who attached the item intended it to become part of the land or building.

Educational Objective 7

7-1. Easements can be created by express words, by implication, or by prescription.

7-2. Examples of profits à prendre include the rights to mine coal, remove sand and gravel, or cut down trees.

7-3. Zoning laws regulate matters such as lot size, minimum building size, number of families that may reside in the buildings, maximum height of each building, and parking areas. Building codes sometimes overlap zoning ordinances but address more technical construction details, such as electrical wiring and heating.

7-4. There are two conditions for granting the petition:

- The land must be taken for public use or public benefit.

- The "Takings Clause" of the Fifth Amendment to the United States Constitution provides that the federal government cannot take private property for public use without paying just compensation to the property owner.

7-5. Bryan can place restrictions on the use of the property as long as those restrictions are not discriminatory or otherwise unenforceable, such as requiring an illegal use. However, state law may limit the restrictions to a period of years, and changed conditions, such as economic conditions in the area, can make the restrictions unenforceable. For example, if the surrounding land had been scenic and rural but then developed into a strip of businesses, including other automobile garages and the like, the restriction might end. Another example would be if employment became depressed in the area and making glue, gun powder, or fertilizers became the most effective economic relief. Such developments could end the restrictions.

Educational Objective 8

8-1. The landlord's primary duty is to deliver possession of the premises to the tenant on the lease's inception date.

8-2. A landlord's remedies against a tenant are the right to evict a tenant or to apply to a court for help in the event of a tenant's breach of lease. The landlord can also seize a tenant's property and hold it for unpaid rent (a right called distraint).

8-3. A tenant's primary right is the right to occupy the premises. A tenant's primary duty is to pay rent and leave the premises in the same condition they were in at the lease inception, except for reasonable wear and tear.

8-4. Landlords are liable for injuries to third parties on the leased premises if the injury is the result of a landlord's negligent acts or latent defects on the premises.

Direct Your Learning

Tort Law

Educational Objectives

After learning the content of this assignment, you should be able to:

1. Describe negligence claims in terms of:
   - The elements of negligence
   - The required proof of negligence

2. Describe these defenses against negligence claims: comparative negligence, releases and exculpatory clauses, immunity, statutes of limitations and repose, and tortfeasor's capacity.

3. Explain how negligence applies to landowners or occupiers of land.

4. Describe these intentional torts, the circumstances under which they can occur, and common defenses to them:
   - Battery
   - Assault
   - False imprisonment and false arrest
   - Intentional infliction of emotional distress
   - Defamation (libel and slander)
   - Invasion of the right of privacy

5. Describe these intentional torts, the circumstances under which they can occur, and common defenses to them:
   - Fraud
   - Bad faith, or outrage
   - Interference with relationships between others
   - Misuse of legal process
   - Trespass

6

- Nuisance
- Conversion

6. Explain how liability attaches as a result of the unique circumstances presented by the following:

    - Ultrahazardous activities
    - Ownership and/or possession of animals
    - Escape of toxic substances

7. Describe these causes of action for products liability and the possible defenses to them:

    - Misrepresentation
    - Breach of warranty
    - Strict liability and negligence

8. Describe the types of damages a court can award a plaintiff for a tort claim.

9. Explain how any of these concepts can affect a tort claim:

    - Joint tortfeasor's liability
    - Expanded liability concepts
    - Vicarious liability
    - Good Samaritan issues
    - Class actions and mass tort litigation

Outline

▶ **Negligence**
- A. Elements of Negligence
  1. Legal Duty
  2. Breach of Duty
  3. Proximate Cause
  4. Actual Injury or Damage
- B. Required Proof of Negligence
  1. Negligence Per Se
  2. Res Ipsa Loquitur

▶ **Defenses Against Negligence Claims**
- A. Comparative Negligence
- B. Releases and Exculpatory Clauses
- C. Immunity
  1. Sovereign, or Governmental, Immunity
  2. Public Official Immunity
  3. Charitable Immunity
  4. Intrafamilial Immunity
- D. Statutes of Limitations and Repose
- E. Tortfeasor's Capacity

▶ **Liability of Landowners or Occupiers of Land**
- A. Natural Conditions
- B. Artificial Conditions
- C. Duties to Those Who Enter the Land or Premises
  1. Licensees
  2. Invitees
  3. Trespassers
  4. Hotel Guests and Tenants

▶ **Intentional Torts: Part 1 of 2**
- A. Battery
- B. Assault
- C. False Imprisonment and False Arrest
- D. Intentional Infliction of Emotional Distress
- E. Defamation (Slander and Libel)
  1. Slander
  2. Libel
  3. Commercial Speech

- F. Invasion of the Right of Privacy
  1. Intrusion on Solitude or Seclusion
  2. Physical Invasion
  3. Torts Involving Use or Disclosure of Information
  4. Defenses to Invasion of Privacy

▶ **Intentional Torts: Part 2 of 2**
- A. Fraud
- B. Bad Faith, or Outrage
  1. Damages
  2. Insurance Cases
  3. Defenses
- C. Interference With Relationships Between Others
  1. Injurious Falsehood
  2. Malicious Interference With Prospective Economic Advantage
  3. Unfair Competition
  4. Interference With Employment
  5. Interference With Copyright, Patent, or Trademark
  6. Interference With Right to Use One's Own Name in Business
  7. Interference With Family Relationships
- D. Misuse of Legal Process
  1. Malicious Prosecution
  2. Malicious Abuse of Process
- E. Trespass
- F. Nuisance
- G. Conversion

▶ **Liability in Extraordinary Circumstances**
- A. Ultrahazardous Activities
- B. Ownership and/or Possession of Animals
- C. Escape of Toxic Substances

▶ **Products Liability**
- A. Misrepresentation
- B. Breach of Warranty
- C. Strict Liability and Negligence
  1. Types of Product Defects
  2. Potentially Liable Parties

 Set aside a specific, realistic amount of time to study every day.

Outline

    3. Parties Protected

    4. Defenses

    5. Damages

▶ **Damages in Tort Suits**

    A. Compensatory Damages

    B. Punitive Damages

    C. Damages for Wrongful Death

▶ **Liability Concepts Affecting Tort Claims**

    A. Joint Tortfeasors

    B. Expanded Liability Concepts

    C. Vicarious Liability

    D. Good Samaritan Issues

    E. Class Actions and Mass Tort Litigation

For each assignment, you should define or describe each of the Key Words and Phrases and answer each of the Review and Application Questions.

Educational Objective 1

Describe negligence claims in terms of:

- **The elements of negligence**
- **The required proof of negligence**

Key Words and Phrases

Tort

Tortfeasor

Plaintiff

Defendant

Legal duty

Statute

Common law (case law)

Reasonable person test

Common carriers

Proximate cause

"But for" rule

Substantial factor rule

Foreseeability rule

Intervening act

Concurrent causation (concurrent causation doctrine)

Negligence per se

Res ipsa loquitur

Exclusive control

Review Questions

1-1. Identify the elements of negligence.

1-2. At the outset of a lawsuit, what presumption favors the defendant?

Educational Objective 2

Describe these defenses against negligence claims: comparative negligence, releases and exculpatory clauses, immunity, statutes of limitations and repose, and tortfeasor's capacity.

Key Words and Phrases

Comparative negligence

Contributory negligence

Last clear chance doctrine

Assumption-of-risk defense

Pure comparative negligence rule

50 percent comparative negligence rule

49 percent comparative negligence rule

Slight versus gross rule

Release

Gross negligence

Immunity

Sovereign immunity (governmental immunity)

Proprietary function

Governmental function

Administrative act (discretionary act)

Ministerial act

Charitable immunity

Interspousal immunity

Parent-child immunity

Statute of limitations

Statute of repose

Review Questions

2-1. Why is the pure comparative negligence rule the maximum departure from the
contributory negligence rule?

2-2. When are exculpatory agreements void?

2-3. Upon what does the extent of public official immunity depend?

Educational Objective 3
Explain how negligence applies to landowners or occupiers of land.

Key Words and Phrases
Trespasser

Nuisance

Attractive nuisance doctrine

Licensee

Invitee

Express license

Implied license

Public invitee

Business invitee

Review Questions

3-1. Would a landowner who digs a deep pit that is difficult to see on his land have a duty to warn trespassers of this condition?

3-2. Does a landlord have a duty to protect tenants from intruders?

Educational Objective 4

Describe these intentional torts, the circumstances under which they can occur, and common defenses to them:

- Battery
- Assault
- False imprisonment and false arrest
- Intentional infliction of emotional distress
- Defamation (libel and slander)
- Invasion of the right of privacy

Key Words and Phrases

Intentional tort

Battery

Assault

False imprisonment

False arrest

Intentional infliction of emotional distress

Negligent infliction of emotional distress

Defamation

Slander

Libel

Publication

Product disparagement, or trade libel

Invasion of privacy

Review Questions

4-1. What is the primary difference between the torts of battery and assault?

4-2. To what do defenses to false imprisonment and false arrest relate?

4-3. What are the defenses for libel and slander?

Educational Objective 5
Describe these intentional torts, the circumstances under which they can occur, and common defenses to them:

- **Fraud**
- **Bad faith, or outrage**
- **Interference with relationships between others**
- **Misuse of legal process**
- **Trespass**
- **Nuisance**
- **Conversion**

Key Words and Phrases
Bad faith (outrage)

Injurious falsehood

Malicious interference with prospective economic advantage

Malice

Unfair competition

Interference with employment

Wrongful-life action

Wrongful-pregnancy action (wrongful-conception action)

Malicious prosecution

Probable cause

Malicious abuse of process

Trespass

Personal property

Private nuisance

Public nuisance

Intentional nuisance

Nuisance per se

Conversion

Review Questions

5-1. In insurance cases, upon what duty is the tort of bad faith based?

5-2. Identify the torts relating to interference with relationships between others.

5-3. How can a defendant defend against a claim of trespass to real or personal property?

Educational Objective 6

Explain how liability attaches as a result of the unique circumstances presented by the following:

- **Ultrahazardous activities**
- **Ownership and/or possession of animals**
- **Escape of toxic substances**

Key Words and Phrases

Strict liability (absolute liability)

Ultrahazardous activity (abnormally dangerous activity)

Toxic tort

Environmental law

Review Questions

6-1. A use or an activity is ultrahazardous or abnormally dangerous under what three circumstances?

6-2. On what basis does the law differentiate between domestic and wild animals for liability questions?

Educational Objective 7

Describe these causes of action for products liability and the possible defenses to them:

- **Misrepresentation**
- **Breach of warranty**
- **Strict liability and negligence**

Key Words and Phrases

Products liability

Express warranty

Implied warranty

Active negligence

Assumption of risk

Passive negligence

Review Questions

7-1. A breach of warranty lawsuit can involve either of what two categories of warranties?

7-2. Contrast the proof required of a plaintiff in a general negligence case involving products liability with that required in a strict liability case involving products liability.

7-3. What factors should a manufacturer consider in deciding whether a product requires a warning of unreasonable danger?

7-4. How do courts determine who has standing to sue in a products liability case?

Educational Objective 8
Describe the types of damages a court can award a plaintiff for a tort claim.

Key Words and Phrases

Special damages

Loss of wages and earnings

General damages

Pain and suffering

Emotional distress

Wrongful death action

Survival statute

Review Questions

8-1.   What basic categories of damages are included in compensatory damages?

8-2.   When can a court award punitive damages?

Educational Objective 9

Explain how any of these concepts can affect a tort claim:

- **Joint tortfeasor's liability**
- **Expanded liability concepts**
- **Vicarious liability**
- **Good Samaritan issues**
- **Class actions and mass tort litigation**

Key Words and Phrases

Joint tortfeasors

Contribution

Enterprise liability (industry-wide liability)

Alternative liability

Market share liability

Concert of action

Conspiracy

Joint venture

Vicarious liability

Negligent entrustment

Negligent supervision

Family purpose doctrine

Good Samaritan law

Class action (class action lawsuit)

Mass tort litigation

Review Questions

9-1. How does the common law differ from a legal trend concerning the application of joint tortfeasor liability?

9-2. What must a plaintiff prove to prevail in a lawsuit under the expanded liability concept of concert of action?

9-3. Identify three relationships that can give rise to vicarious liability.

Answers to Assignment 6 Questions

NOTE: These answers are provided to give students a basic understanding of acceptable types of responses. They often are not the only valid answers and are not intended to provide an exhaustive response to the questions.

Educational Objective 1

1-1. The elements of negligence are that the defendant owed a legal duty of care to the plaintiff; the defendant breached that duty; the defendant's negligent act was the proximate cause of the plaintiff's injury or damage; and the plaintiff suffered actual injury or damage.

1-2. At the outset of a lawsuit, the defendant is presumed to have used due care until the plaintiff proves otherwise.

Educational Objective 2

2-1. The pure comparative negligence rule is the maximum departure from the contributory negligence rule because a plaintiff who is as much as 99 percent at fault can still recover 1 percent of the claimed damages.

2-2. Exculpatory agreements are void if they exclude willful or wanton misconduct.

2-3. The extent of public official immunity depends on whether the acts are administrative or ministerial acts.

Educational Objective 3

3-1. Yes. A landowner creating an artificial condition on land that could cause severe injury or death has a duty to warn of the hazard if a trespasser probably would not discover it without warning.

3-2. Under common law, the landlord was under no duty to protect tenants from intruders. However, many courts now impose a duty on landlords, hotel operators, and public entities to take reasonable precautions to secure their premises against foreseeable risks of harm by intruders.

Educational Objective 4

4-1. Battery requires touching, but assault does not involve touching.

4-2. Defenses to false imprisonment and false arrest relate to whether the acts occurred in connection with a crime, the nature of the crime, and the capacity of the individual involved.

4-3. The defenses for libel and slander are that the statement was true; that the defendant made or printed a retraction (partial defense); and that the statement had an absolute, conditional, or qualified privilege.

Educational Objective 5

5-1. In insurance cases, the tort of bad faith is based on an insurer's implied duty to act fairly and in good faith in discharging its duties under an insurance contract.

5-2. The torts relating to interference with relationships between others are injurious falsehood; malicious interference with prospective economic advantage; unfair competition; interference with employment; interference with copyright, patent, or trademark; interference with the right to use one's own name in business; and interference with family relationships.

5-3. A defendant can defend against a claim of trespass to real or personal property by alleging that the plaintiff did not own or possess the property, that the plaintiff consented to the defendant's entry, or that the defendant did not enter onto or take control of the property.

Educational Objective 6

6-1. A use or an activity is ultrahazardous or abnormally dangerous under these circumstances:

- It has a high degree of risk of serious harm.

- It cannot be performed without the high degree of risk.

- It does not normally occur in the area in which it is conducted.

6-2. The law differentiates between domestic and wild animals based on local custom.

Educational Objective 7

7-1. A breach of warranty lawsuit can involve either an express warranty or an implied warranty.

7-2. In a general negligence case involving products liability, the plaintiff must prove that the manufacturer failed to use reasonable care in designing or manufacturing the product that caused the injury. In a strict liability case, proof of either negligence or an intent to harm is not required. The manufacturer's conduct is irrelevant, and the focus is on the product itself.

7-3. A manufacturer should consider three factors in relation to warning about a product's danger:

- Degree of the danger

- Knowledge of the danger

- Foreseeability of dangerous use

7-4. In determining who has legal standing to sue, most courts use the traditional foreseeability test. Anyone who could foreseeably have been injured by the product has standing to sue.

Educational Objective 8

8-1. Compensatory damages include special and general damages.

8-2. A court can award punitive damages when a defendant actually intended to cause harm or acted oppressively, maliciously, or fraudulently.

Educational Objective 9

9-1. Under common law, joint tortfeasors were jointly and severally liable for the full amount of the damages. About half the jurisdictions have abolished this rule—today, they do not hold a joint tortfeasor automatically liable for all of a plaintiff's damages.

9-2. Under the expanded liability concept of concert of action, a plaintiff must prove either (1) that the defendants consciously parallel each other as the result of an actual agreement or an implied understanding to do or not to do a given act, or (2) that, even though the defendants acted independently, the effect of their acts was to encourage or assist others' wrongful conduct.

9-3. The principal and agent, employer and employee, and parent and child relationships can all give rise to vicarious liability.

Direct Your Learning

Agency Law

Educational Objectives

After learning the content of this assignment, you should be able to:

1. Explain how an agency relationship can be created by each of the following:

   - Appointment

   - Estoppel

   - Ratification

2. Describe an agent's authority in terms of the following:

   - The scope of authority granted (actual or apparent)

   - The third party's duty to ascertain scope of authority

3. Describe the principal-agent relationship in terms of the following:

   - Duties an agent owes to the principal

   - Remedies a principal has for an agent's breach of duties

   - Duties a principal owes to an agent

   - Remedies an agent has for a principal's breach of duties

4. Describe the various means by which parties can terminate agency relationships.

5. Describe the potential contractual rights and liabilities of a principal and its agent in terms of the following:

   - A third party's rights against a principal

   - A principal's rights against a third party

   - An agent's liability to a third party

   - An agent's rights against a third party

7

6. Describe the potential tort liability of a principal and its agent in terms of the following:

   - Respondeat superior liability of the principal for the agent's torts
   - Direct liability of the principal for the agent's torts
   - Principal's liability for torts of independent contractors
   - Principal's liability for agent's misrepresentations
   - Agent's liability for agent's own torts

Outline

▶ **Agency Creation**
  A. Appointment
  B. Estoppel
  C. Ratification

▶ **Agent's Authority**
  A. Scope of Authority
    1. Actual Authority
    2. Apparent Authority
  B. Duty to Ascertain Scope of Authority

▶ **Agent's Duties and Remedies**
  A. Agent's Duties to Principal
    1. Loyalty
    2. Obedience
    3. Reasonable Care
    4. Accounting
    5. Information
  B. Principal's Remedies
  C. Principal's Duties to Agent
    1. Agreed-On Period of Employment
    2. Compensation
    3. Reimbursement for Expenses
    4. Indemnity for Losses
  D. Agent's Remedies

▶ **Agency Termination**
  A. Just Cause
  B. Lapse of Time
  C. Accomplishment of Purpose
  D. Revocation
  E. Renunciation
  F. Death or Incapacity
  G. Changed Circumstances

▶ **Contractual Rights and Liabilities**
  A. Third Party's Rights Against a Principal
  B. Principal's Rights Against a Third Party
  C. Agent's Liability to a Third Party
  D. Agent's Rights Against a Third Party

▶ **Tort Liability of Principal and Agent**
  A. Principal's Liability for Agent's Torts
    1. Respondeat Superior Liability
    2. Direct Liability
    3. Liability for Independent Contractor's Torts
    4. Liability for Agent's Misrepresentations
  B. Agent's Liability for Own Torts

Reward yourself after you reach specific goals.

For each assignment, you should define or describe each of the Key Words and Phrases and answer each of the Review and Application Questions.

Educational Objective 1

Explain how an agency relationship can be created by each of the following:

- **Appointment**
- **Estoppel**
- **Ratification**

Key Words and Phrases

Agency

Agent

Principal

Power of attorney

Agency by estoppel

Ratification

Review Questions

1-1. Identify the usual method of creating an agency.

1-2. Explain how an agency by estoppel can be created even though the principal has done nothing to create the agency.

1-3. Contrast ratification with estoppel as it relates to the law of agency.

Educational Objective 2

Describe an agent's authority in terms of the following:

- **The scope of authority granted (actual or apparent)**
- **The third party's duty to ascertain scope of authority**

Key Words and Phrases

Actual authority

Express authority

Implied authority

Apparent authority

Review Questions

2-1. Compare an agent's express and implied authority.

2-2. Contrast apparent authority with actual authority.

2-3. Explain a third party's duty to ascertain the scope of an agent's authority.

Application Question

2-4. Brittany has been employed by High End Jewelry for two weeks as a sales clerk. Brittany is permitted to make transactions when customers pay by cash or major credit card. She is not permitted to extend store credit. All applications for store credit go to Helen, the sales manager, for approval. Brittany's friend Jodie comes into the store and admires a diamond tennis bracelet that costs $1,500. Brittany tells Jodie she will let her have it for a deposit of $50 and a completed credit application for the balance of $1,450. Brittany tells Jodie she can pay $25 per month. Jodie, who has no job except for babysitting, completes the credit application. Is High End bound to extend the credit to Jodie for the bracelet?

Educational Objective 3

Describe the principal-agent relationship in terms of the following:

- **Duties an agent owes to the principal**
- **Remedies a principal has for an agent's breach of duties**
- **Duties a principal owes to an agent**
- **Remedies an agent has for a principal's breach of duties**

Key Word or Phrase

Ministerial duties

Review Questions

3-1. List the duties an agent owes to a principal.

3-2. List three exceptions to the rule that an agent cannot delegate to another the authority granted by a principal.

3-3. List the duties a principal owes to an agent.

3-4. Describe the agent's remedies for a principal's breach of duties.

Educational Objective 4
Describe the various means by which parties can terminate agency relationships.

Review Questions

4-1.   How does a principal revoke an agency?

4-2.   List three ways in which an agency may be terminated by death or incapacity.

4-3.   Under what circumstances does appointment of a second agent to accomplish the authorized agency purpose terminate the original agency?

Educational Objective 5

Describe the potential contractual rights and liabilities of a principal and its agent in terms of the following:

- A third party's rights against a principal
- A principal's rights against a third party
- An agent's liability to a third party
- An agent's rights against a third party

Key Words and Phrases

Disclosed principal

Partially disclosed principal

Review Questions

5-1.   Explain why a third party can sue an undisclosed principal once that principal's existence becomes apparent.

5-2.   Describe the circumstances under which a third party's rights against a principal are discharged.

5-3. Describe the rights of a third party who pays money to an agent who has no authority to collect it.

5-4. Explain why an agent is liable to a third party for a fraudulent or malicious act that harms the third party.

Educational Objective 6

Describe the potential tort liability of a principal and its agent in terms of the following:

- **Respondeat superior liability of the principal for the agent's torts**
- **Direct liability of the principal for the agent's torts**
- **Principal's liability for torts of independent contractors**
- **Principal's liability for agent's misrepresentations**
- **Agent's liability for agent's own torts**

Key Words and Phrases

Employee

Independent contractor

Respondeat superior

Joint and several liability

Review Questions

6-1. Describe the two conditions that must be met in order for the torts of an agent to be vicariously attributed to the principal.

6-2. Describe the elements required to determine whether an employee was acting within the scope of his or her employment when a tort was committed.

6-3. Describe the principal's responsibility for hiring, training, and supervising agents.

6-4. Identify three exceptions to the rule that a principal is not liable for the torts of agents that are independent contractors.

Answers to Assignment 7 Questions

NOTE: These answers are provided to give students a basic understanding of acceptable types of responses. They often are not the only valid answers and are not intended to provide an exhaustive response to the questions.

Educational Objective 1

1-1. The usual method of creating an agency is by express appointment.

1-2. If a principal's words or conduct cause a third person to reasonably believe that an agency exists and to rely on that representation in dealing with the supposed agent, the principal is estopped (prevented) from denying the agency, resulting in agency by estoppel.

1-3. Ratification establishes the agency relationship. An estoppel does not create an agency relationship but only protects the third person from a loss that would result if the agency were denied.

Educational Objective 2

2-1. An agent's actual authority can be express or implied. Express authority applies to carrying out the principal's specific instructions and performing acts incident to carrying out those instructions. The most common source of implied authority is custom. Without different instructions, an agent's authority extends to, and is limited to, what a person in this agent's position usually does. Implied authority can also apply when an agent acts beyond the usual scope of authority in an emergency.

2-2. Unlike actual authority, a principal neither confers apparent authority on an agent nor creates it. Apparent authority is based on appearances and includes all the authority that a reasonable person, acquainted with the customs and nature of the business, could reasonably assume the agent has.

2-3. A third party is not entitled to rely on an agent's statements about the scope of the agent's authority. Only the actual authority the principal has given, or the apparent authority the principal has manifested to the third party, controls the extent of the agent's authority. If an agent acts in a way adverse to the principal's best interests, the third party has notice that the agent might be exceeding his or her authority. The third party must ascertain the scope of the agent's authority by a direct inquiry to the principal. If the third party fails to inquire, and the agent does not have authority, the transaction in question does not bind the principal.

2-4. High End is not bound to extend the credit to Jodie. A reasonable person would realize that Brittany did not have the authority to extend credit in this situation.

Educational Objective 3

3-1. An agent's implied duties to a principal include these:

- Loyalty

- Obedience

- Reasonable care

- Accounting

- Information

3-2. These three exceptions apply to the nondelegation rule:

- Ministerial duties—If certain tasks do not require judgment or discretion, an agent can delegate their performance.

- Customary appointments—If custom and usage of a particular business involve the delegation of authority, the agent can delegate.

- Emergency appointments—In an emergency that requires the appointment of another to protect the principal's interests, the agent can make an emergency appointment.

3-3. The principal owes these duties to the agent:

- Agreed-on period of employment

- Compensation

- Reimbursement for expenses

- Indemnity for losses

3-4. An agent can sue for compensation, indemnity, or reimbursement and can also obtain a court order requiring an accounting from the principal. An agent discharged by a principal during a specified employment period can sue for compensation for the remainder of the period. An agent can also exercise a lien, or right to retain possession of the principal's goods, until the principal has paid the amounts due.

Educational Objective 4

4-1. To revoke an agency, the principal notifies the agent, by word or act, that the agent no longer has authority.

4-2. Death or incapacity can terminate an agency in these ways:

- The death of either principal or agent terminates the agency.

- The incapacity of the principal terminates the agency.

- The principal has the right to terminate the agency upon learning of the agent's incapacity.

4-3. If the principal appoints another agent to accomplish the authorized purpose, and if the new appointment conflicts with the first, the original agent's authority is terminated.

Educational Objective 5

5-1. An undisclosed principal is responsible for all contracts the agent enters into within the scope of the agent's actual authority. The third party can sue the principal when the principal's existence becomes apparent. Because the principal was originally unknown to the third party, the principal could not have created any apparent authority.

5-2. A third party cannot sue the principal if, having learned of both the principal's existence and the principal's identity, the third party expresses the intention to hold the agent liable for the contract. Election of the agent discharges the principal.

5-3. If a third party pays money to an agent who has no authority to collect it and the agent does not turn the money over to the principal, the third party can sue the agent for the money. The agent cannot avoid liability by subsequently paying wrongfully collected funds to a principal.

5-4. An agent who wrongfully injures a third party or is guilty of theft is personally liable. The fact that the agent was acting in good faith under the principal's direction is not a defense against personal tort or criminal liability.

Educational Objective 6

6-1. The two conditions that must be met are:

- The agent must be an employee of the principal.

- The tort must be committed while the agent is acting within the scope of his or her employment.

6-2. Generally, agents are considered to be acting in the scope of employment if they are performing work assigned by the employer or undertaking activities subject to the employer's control. The critical element is that the employer controls or has the right to control how the agent performs the assigned work.

6-3. The principal is responsible for selecting appropriate individuals as agents; giving them clear instructions; providing them with appropriate tools, equipment, or materials; monitoring their performance; and discharging those that do not perform appropriately.

6-4. The three exceptions to the rule that principals are not liable for the torts of independent contractors are these:

- A principal who negligently enters into an agency with an independent contractor that is unsuitable or incompetent can be held liable for resulting harm to third parties.

- Certain duties are considered so important that responsibility for them cannot be delegated to another party. If a principal hires an independent contractor to perform one of these important duties and the contractor fails to perform or performs inadequately, the principal may be liable for any resulting harm or damage to third parties.

- A principal who hires an independent contractor to perform highly dangerous activities—for example, building demolition—must ensure that the contractor takes appropriate safety precautions.

Direct Your Learning

Agency Law: Insurance Applications

Educational Objectives

After learning the content of this assignment, you should be able to:

1. Describe the agency relationship that exists between insurers and each classification of producers:

   - Agents

   - Brokers

2. Distinguish a producer's actual authority, both express and implied, from apparent authority.

3. Explain how the extent of a producer's authority is affected by these factors:

   - Producers' status as general agents, special agents, or brokers

   - Producers' notice and knowledge

   - Producers' authority to bind coverage

   - Appointment of subagents

4. Explain how producers' authority can be terminated.

5. Describe producers' duties and liabilities to insurance customers, third parties, and insurers.

Outline

▶ **Insurance Producer Classifications**

   A. Agents

   B. Brokers

▶ **Producers' Authority**

   A. Actual Authority

   B. Apparent Authority

▶ **Extent of Producers' Authority**

   A. Producers' Status as General Agents, Special Agents, or Brokers

   B. Producers' Notice and Knowledge

   C. Producers' Authority to Bind Coverage

   D. Appointment of Subagents

▶ **Termination of Producer Authority**

▶ **Producers' Duties and Liabilities**

   A. Producers' Duties and Liability to Insurance Customers

      1. Producer's Duty to Follow Instructions

      2. Producer's Duty to Procure Insurance

      3. Producer's Duty to Maintain Coverage

      4. Producer's Duty to Place Insurance With a Solvent Insurer

      5. Producer's Duty to Advise

   B. Producers' Defenses to Liability

      1. Producer Assumed No Duty to Customer

      2. Producer Did Not Breach Duty to Customer

      3. Insurance Customer Was Partly at Fault

      4. Insurance Customer Failed to Read Policy

      5. Insurance Was Not Available to the Customer

   C. Producers' Duties and Liabilities to Third Parties

   D. Producers' Duties and Liability to Insurer

      1. Duty to Disclose Risks

      2. Duty to Follow Instructions

      3. Duties of Loyalty and Accounting

      4. Duty to Transmit Information Properly

Studying before sleeping helps you retain material better than studying before undertaking other tasks.

For each assignment, you should define or describe each of the Key Words and Phrases and answer each of the Review and Application Questions.

Educational Objective 1

Describe the agency relationship that exists between insurers and each classification of producers:

- **Agents**
- **Brokers**

Key Words and Phrases

Insurance producer

Insurance agent

General agent

Special agent

Soliciting agent

Broker

Review Questions

1-1.   Compare the degree of discretion the three categories of agents—general agent, special agent, and soliciting agent—have in carrying out their functions.

1-2.   Contrast the roles of insurance agent and insurance broker.

1-3.   Describe the roles of insurance brokers.

Educational Objective 2

Distinguish a producer's actual authority, both express and implied, from apparent authority.

Review Questions

2-1.   Describe actual authority in regard to insurance producers.

2-2. Compare an insurance producer's express authority with implied authority.

2-3. Describe apparent authority of insurance producers.

2-4. Describe the two types of circumstances that usually give rise to apparent authority for insurance producers.

Application Question

2-5. Wanda owns a busy insurance agency in a small rural town and represents several insurers, one of which is InsureCo. Two clients, Manny and Jill, recently purchased a small farm with an area for producing honey, and Wanda arranged insurance coverage with InsureCo for the farm. InsureCo is an independent filer and uses its own forms, which appear to Wanda to be similar to the standard forms. There is nothing stated on InsureCo's forms regarding agent authority. Jill asks Wanda whether her bees will be covered. Wanda, who is familiar with the ISO Farm Personal Property Coverage Form, assures her that her bees will be covered for any covered cause of loss. A few months after the policy is issued, there is a severe storm that results in a total loss of Jill's beehives and bees, along with other property damage on the farm. InsureCo covers the other damage, but refuses to cover the loss of the bees because there is an exclusion in its policy for bees. Did Wanda have authority to tell Jill that her bees would be covered by her InsureCo policy?

Educational Objective 3

Explain how the extent of a producer's authority is affected by these factors:

- Producers' status as general agents, special agents, or brokers
- Producers' notice and knowledge
- Producers' authority to bind coverage
- Appointment of subagents

Review Questions

3-1. Compare the extent of authority for the different types of insurance producers—general agents, special agents, and brokers.

3-2. Compare the typical insurance duties of a general agent and a broker.

3-3. Describe the two instances in which a broker can be both an agent and insured's representative.

3-4. Describe imputed knowledge in the agent-insurer relationship.

   a.   Is there imputed knowledge in the broker-insurer relationship?

   b.   Is there imputed knowledge if an agent is aware that information provided by an insured was false?

   c.   Is there imputed knowledge if an insured provides false information with-
        out the agent being aware that the information is false?

3-5. Describe the typical authority of insurance producers to issue temporary oral or
      written policies.

3-6. Explain whether apparent authority applies to an insurance producer's sub-
      agents.

Application Question

3-7. While Julio, a general insurance agent for InsureCo, is out of the office, his assistant binds auto coverage for Limo, a small limousine company. Julio has authority to bind coverage for InsureCo but has not given his assistant this authority. However, the assistant knows the agency is struggling to meet its sales goal for the month and believes that this business will help the agency reach its goal. The assistant is not aware of a memo Julio received from InsureCo that it prefers not to write any additional limousine business. The day after Julio's assistant binds coverage, there is a serious accident involving one of Limo's vehicles. Explain whether InsureCo is liable for this loss.

Educational Objective 4

Explain how producers' authority can be terminated.

Review Questions

4-1. How does an insurance producer/insurer agency relationship terminate?

4-2. Describe the typical termination procedures that end a producer's authority.

4-3. Explain how apparent authority can arise after termination of a producer/insurer agency relationship.

4-4. Describe methods an insurer can use to prevent a producer's exercise of apparent authority after termination of the producer/insurer agency relationship.

Application Question

4-5. InsureCo's contract with the Small Agency expires on June 30, and InsureCo elects not to renew the contract because of dissatisfaction with the book of business produced by Small. InsureCo sends written notice to Small of the contract expiration and the termination of the contract's express authority to bind coverage. However, InsureCo does not notify any of Small's customers. High Risk, a customer of Small and InsureCo, has coverage expire on July 15. Small tells High Risk that Small will get its coverage renewed and submits the renewal to InsureCo. Explain whether InsureCo is bound to provide coverage to High Risk.

Educational Objective 5

Describe producers' duties and liabilities to insurance customers, third parties, and insurers.

Review Questions

5-1. Describe the standard of care and skill that is required of insurance producers and the five duties that producers owe their customers.

5-2. Describe liabilities that could result from a producer's failure to follow instructions.

5-3. Contrast a producer's duty to procure insurance with the duty to follow instructions.

5-4. Describe the extent of an agent's duty to determine an insurer's solvency.

5-5. Explain why an insured's failure to read the policy is not always an adequate producer defense against liability.

5-6. Describe the liability of an insurance producer to an insurer for failing to fully disclose information regarding a prospective insured.

    a. Describe the producer's liability if the insurer would not have issued a policy to the insured if the producer had fully disclosed the risks and hazards.

    b. Describe the producer's liability if the insurer would have issued the policy but with a higher premium.

Application Question

5-7. Paul, an insurance broker, procures a workers compensation insurance policy for Pipefitters. Dan, the owner of Pipefitters, tells Paul that he has begun work in a nearby state. Paul procures a policy with coverage in the state of Pipefitters' home office, where Paul's office is also located, and this state is listed on the policy's information page. Paul delivers a copy of the policy to Dan a week after the effective date. The policy states that if there is work in another state not listed on the information page as of the effective date of the policy, coverage will not be afforded for that state unless the insurer is notified within thirty days. Sixty-one days after the effective date of the policy, an employee of Pipefitters is seriously injured in an accident at the operation in the nearby state. The insurer denies coverage because it is outside the state listed on the information page of the policy. The insurer tells Dan that no notice was provided to them of the operation in that state.

a. Is the insurer responsible to pay the loss?

b. Is Paul, the producer, liable for the loss?

c. Can Paul use the defense that Dan failed to read the policy?

d. Does the injured employee have a right of action against Paul?

Answers to Assignment 8 Questions

NOTE: These answers are provided to give students a basic understanding of acceptable types of responses. They often are not the only valid answers and are not intended to provide an exhaustive response to the questions.

Educational Objective 1

1-1. A general agent has broad powers within underwriting guidelines. A special agent has more restricted authority than a general agent; it is restricted by express agreement with an insurer. A soliciting agent has narrow authority derived directly from an agency contract.

1-2. An insurance agent represents an insurer. An insurance broker usually represents an insurance customer.

1-3. An insurance broker typically helps large insureds obtain coverage from competing insurers. Some insurance brokers have expanded their roles to become risk consultants who advise clients how to handle their loss exposures. Brokers may also offer risk control or claims services, or assist insurers in obtaining reinsurance coverage.

Educational Objective 2

2-1. Actual authority is that which the principal (insurer) intentionally confers upon the producer or allows the producer to believe he or she possesses.

2-2. Typically, express authority is granted through a formal written contract that establishes the terms of the principal/agent relationship between the insurance producer and the insurer. This agency contract states the producer's powers and authority and specifies any restrictions on that authority. The parties, however, can agree to a relationship by less formal means, creating implied authority. For example, an agent's submission of an insurance application can create an agency relationship if the producer has solicited and forwarded insurance applications to the insurer previously, and the insurer has accepted them.

2-3. An insurer does not give apparent authority to the producer (nor does the producer create this authority), but appearances may lead a third party to believe that a producer has authority.

2-4. Apparent authority usually arises in one of two overlapping circumstances. First, an insurer may grant less actual authority to the producer than producers in the same position in that business usually have. Second, the method of operation of the principal's business differs from the method of operation of other businesses of the same kind in the principal's area.

2-5. Wanda likely had apparent authority to tell Manny and Jill that their bees would be covered by InsureCo. InsureCo differs from the other insurers Wanda represents by not using the standard ISO policy forms. Wanda's authority from most of the insurers she represents includes binding coverage. Because Wanda appeared to Manny and Jill to have authority to represent InsureCo's coverage, and because the coverage for bees was typical of farm insurance policies issued in that town, Wanda likely had apparent authority from InsureCo to make representations regarding that coverage.

Educational Objective 3

3-1. The extent of a producer's authority varies depending on whether the producer is a general agent, special agent, or broker. The general agent represents an insurer and has the broadest authority of all insurance agents. Any action the general agent takes according to the agreed-on authority binds the insurer. A special agent's authority is usually restricted to soliciting and forwarding prospective business to an insurer. Any action the special agent takes beyond soliciting and forwarding business will usually not bind an insurer unless an insured can establish apparent authority. A broker has no authority to act on behalf of an insurer because brokers represent insureds, not insurers. A broker typically has authority to bind an insured.

3-2. General agents typically can accept loss exposures, agree on and settle the terms of insurance, waive policy provisions, issue and renew policies, collect premiums, and adjust claims. A broker's typical duties include procuring insurance for the insurance customer-principal, selecting the insurer to provide the desired coverage, arranging for the payment of premiums, canceling and receiving unearned premiums on a policy the broker has obtained, and obtaining a new policy upon cancellation of one previously obtained.

3-3. First, through apparent authority, the broker is legally the insurer's agent if the insurer allows the broker to act in a manner leading a reasonable third party to believe that the broker is the insurer's agent. Second, some state statutes provide that, for specific purposes, such as receipt of premium payments, a broker is the insurer's agent.

3-4. In agency law, any knowledge possessed by an agent, general or special, is considered to be possessed by that agent's principal as well. In an insurance context, the authorized agent's knowledge is imputed to the insurer—whether the insurer actually receives the information from the agent is irrelevant.

    a.   An agent's knowledge is not imputed to an insurer if no agency relationship exists between them. Under most circumstances, an insurance broker's knowledge is not imputed. The broker's agency relationship is with the insured, not the insurer.

    b.   The agent's decision to act adversely to the insurer's interests breaks the agency relationship, which is the basis of the imputed knowledge rule.

    c.   If an agent is unaware that information provided by an insurance customer is false, no knowledge is imputed to the insurer. The insurer can avoid liability under the policy if it can prove fraud or misrepresentation.

3-5. The need for immediate insurance coverage arises frequently. However, insurers usually undertake an underwriting process that can take several weeks or longer to complete before issuing a policy. Because this delay leaves applicants unprotected, many insurers authorize producers to issue temporary oral or written policies pending acceptance of the application.

3-6. The doctrine of apparent authority can apply to subagents. To the public, an insurance producer's subagents appear to have authorization to act for the insurer, even when they do not have such authority. In many such circumstances, these subagents' acts bind the insurer under the doctrine of apparent authority.

3-7. InsureCo is most likely liable for Limo's loss. Julio had authority from InsureCo to bind coverage. Although Julio's assistant had not been granted this authority, the general public, including Limo, could not be aware of the limits on the assistant's authority. The assistant thus had apparent authority, and InsureCo is bound by the actions of this agency employee.

Educational Objective 4

4-1. A producer/insurer agency relationship usually terminates under circumstances specified in the contract. The relationship can also terminate when one of the parties acts in a way that the other party might reasonably construe as showing the intent to terminate. The agency relationship can also terminate by other means, including operation of law, the producer's death or insanity, or the insurer's insolvency.

4-2. Typically, termination occurs through a written or oral communication, which severs the producer's actual authority to bind the insurance principal.

4-3. If a third party who has dealt with the producer does not receive notification of the termination, the producer's acts might bind the insurer. The producer can also bind the insurer regarding third parties with whom he or she has not dealt with previously if these parties had prior knowledge of the former agency relationship but no notice of the termination.

4-4. The safest way for an insurer to avoid the possible adverse consequences of apparent authority is for the insurer to notify all third parties known to have dealt with the producer and repossess from the producer any evidence of the agency relationship, such as application forms and insurer stationery.

4-5. InsureCo is likely bound to provide coverage to High Risk. Although InsureCo terminated Small Agency's agency contract and authority by written communication to Small, InsureCo did not notify any of Small's customers that the producer relationship had ended. Therefore, High Risk has no knowledge of the termination of the agency relationship, and Small has apparent authority to bind coverage.

Educational Objective 5

5-1. Insurance producers have a duty to exercise reasonable care and skill in performing their duties, to deal with their customers in good faith, and to exercise reasonable diligence on their customers' behalf. They also have a duty to have reasonable knowledge about the insurance policies they sell, the policy terms, and the coverages available in the areas for which their customers seek insurance protection. Insurance producers also have a duty to follow their customers' instructions.

There are five duties that producers owe their customers:

- Duty to follow instructions
- Duty to procure insurance
- Duty to maintain coverage
- Duty to place insurance with a solvent insurer
- Duty to advise

5-2. A producer must strictly follow the customer's instructions and is liable to the customer for any damages that result from not doing so. A producer who fails to add an available coverage requested by an insured is liable for a subsequent loss that the policy would have covered had the producer followed instructions. Also, a producer who fails to add newly acquired property to the list of the insured's covered properties at the insured's request would be liable for the financial consequences resulting from any uninsured loss involving the property.

5-3. The duty to follow instructions may involve nondiscretionary acts. However, the duty to procure insurance involves care, skill, effort, and diligence on the insurance producer's part. The producer has a duty not only to procure insurance, but also to procure the appropriate coverage.

5-4. The producer should make reasonable attempts to inquire into prospective insurers' solvency and should disclose to the customer any information revealing a weak financial condition. The producer should also document any disclosures made to a customer regarding an insurer's solvency.

5-5. Some state courts do not allow this defense, reasoning that the customer has the right to rely on the producer's expertise and that policy language is often difficult to understand.

5-6. An insurance producer who fails to fully disclose all material information concerning the risks and hazards of a prospective insured is liable to the insurer for damages resulting from the lack of full disclosure.

   a. If the insurer establishes that it would not have issued the policy had it received the appropriate information, the producer is liable to the insurer for the amount of the loss the insurer must pay to the insured.

   b. If the insurer would have issued the policy but with a higher premium, the producer would be liable to the insurer for the difference in the premium.

5-7. The responsibilities held by each of the parties will be decided by the contract in these ways:

   a. The insurer is not responsible to pay the loss. The insurer was not notified of the operation in the nearby state as required by the policy provisions.

   b. Paul, the producer, is liable for the loss. Paul had a duty to Dan and Pipefitters to procure appropriate coverage. Dan informed Paul of his new operation, and Paul had a duty to procure coverage appropriate for all of Dan's operations and employees.

   c. Paul is not likely to be successful in a defense that Dan did not read the policy. Dan described his operations to Paul, and Paul delivered the policy to Dan. As a producer, Paul is presumed to be professional and knowledgeable about the insurance products he markets, and he has a duty to procure appropriate coverage.

   d. Under general contract law principles, the parties to an agreement owe duties and obligations to each other, but not to third parties. That the third party could have collected had the producer discharged all duties appropriately, but now cannot collect, usually does not give the third party any rights against the producer. However, some courts have recognized the third-party right of injured workers to sue producers for failure to discharge a duty to procure workers compensation coverage because of the importance of injured workers receiving compensation and because workers are the intended beneficiaries of workers compensation or employer's liability insurance.

Direct Your Learning

Employment Law and Business Entities

Educational Objectives

After learning the content of this assignment, you should be able to:

1. Describe the employment-at-will doctrine and its exceptions.

2. Summarize the laws prohibiting discrimination on the basis of each of the following:

   - Age

   - Sex, race, color, religion, or national origin

   - Disability

   - Other factors

3. Summarize the laws governing labor-management relations in terms of the following:

   - Collective-bargaining relationships

   - Collective-bargaining process

   - Economic pressures

4. Summarize the laws that protect employees' rights in the following areas:

   - Employee safety and health

   - Employee wages and hours

   - Family medical leave

   - Employee benefits

   - Employee privacy

5. When contemplating incorporation, explain how each of the following would factor into the decision:

   - Advantages of incorporation

   - Federal and state regulation of corporations

9

- Foreign corporations

- Incorporation process

- Corporate ownership

6. Explain the rights, duties, powers, obligations, and liabilities of a corporation and the corporation's directors, officers, and stockholders.

7. Describe the procedures by which corporate existence can terminate through merger, dissolution, and reorganization.

8. Describe the characteristics, purposes, and functions of the following:

   - Partnerships

   - Limited partnerships

   - Limited liability partnerships

   - Limited liability companies

9. Describe the characteristics, purpose, and functions of unincorporated associations.

Outline

▶ **Employment at Will**

  A. Employment-at-Will Doctrine

  B. Public Policy Exception

  C. Implied-Contract Exception

  D. Covenant-of-Good-Faith Exception

  E. Statutory Exception

▶ **Antidiscrimination Laws**

  A. Discrimination Based on Age

     1. Age Discrimination in Employment Act (ADEA)

     2. Older Workers Benefit Protection Act (OWBPA)

  B. Discrimination Based on Sex, Race, Color, Religion, or National Origin

     1. Civil Rights Acts of 1866 and 1871

     2. Civil Rights Act of 1964

     3. Civil Rights Act of 1991

     4. Executive Order 11246

     5. Equal Pay Act

     6. Immigration Reform and Control Act of 1986

  C. Discrimination Based on Disability

     1. Rehabilitation Act of 1973

     2. Americans With Disabilities Act

  D. Discrimination Based on Other Factors

▶ **Labor-Management Relations**

  A. Collective-Bargaining Relationships

     1. Norris-LaGuardia Act of 1932 and National Labor Relations Act (NLRA) of 1935

     2. Exclusive Bargaining Agent

  B. Collective-Bargaining Process

  C. Economic Pressure

     1. Union Economic Tactics

     2. Employer Economic Tactics

▶ **Employee Welfare Laws**

  A. Regulation of Employee Safety and Health

  B. Regulation of Employee Wages and Hours

  C. Family Medical Leave Act

  D. Regulation of Employee Benefits

     1. Employee Retirement Income Security Act (ERISA)

     2. Consolidated Omnibus Budget Reconciliation Act (COBRA)

     3. Health Care and Education Reconciliation Act of 2010

  E. Employee Privacy

     1. Privacy Statutes

     2. Health Insurance Portability and Accountability Act (HIPAA)

▶ **Corporations: Formation**

  A. Advantages of Incorporation

  B. Federal and State Laws and Regulations

  C. Foreign Corporations

  D. Incorporation Process

  E. Corporate Ownership

     1. Stock

     2. Board of Directors

▶ **Corporations: Duties and Obligations**

  A. Corporate Powers

  B. Liability for Torts and Crimes

  C. Duties of Directors and Officers

     1. Duties of Care and Loyalty

     2. Transactions With the Corporation

     3. Appropriation of a Corporate Business Opportunity

  D. Stockholders' Powers and Duties

     1. Stockholders' Meetings

     2. Stockholders' Actions

  E. Dividends

▶ **Corporations: Mergers, Dissolution, and Reorganization**

  A. Merger

     1. Share Exchange and De Facto Mergers

     2. Takeovers and Tender Offers

  B. Dissolution

  C. Reorganization

▶ **Partnerships**

  A. Partnership Formation

  B. Partnership Liability

When reviewing for your exam, remember to allot time for frequent breaks.

Outline

C. Partners' Relationships to One Another

1. Financial Relationship

2. Fiduciary Relationship

3. Partnerships' Books and Property

4. Assignment of Partner's Interest in Partnership

D. Relationships of Partners to Third Parties

1. Apparent Authority (Estoppel) of Partners

2. Acts Outside the Usual Scope of Business

3. Ability to Convey Real Property

E. Dissolution, Winding Up, and Termination

1. Rightful and Wrongful Dissolution

2. Winding Up the Partnership Business

3. Effect of Dissolution on Third Parties

F. Limited Partnerships and Limited Liability Partnerships

G. Limited Liability Companies

▶ Unincorporated Associations

A. Characteristics of Unincorporated Associations

1. State Regulation

2. Types of Associations

B. Formation and Financing

1. Articles of Association and Bylaws

2. Rights of Members in Association Property

3. Directors or Trustees

C. Liability of Members to Third Parties

D. Dissolution and Winding Up

For each assignment, you should define or describe each of the Key Words and Phrases and answer each of the Review and Application Questions.

Educational Objective 1
Describe the employment-at-will doctrine and its exceptions.

Key Words and Phrases

Wrongful discharge

Common-law system

Review Questions

1-1. Describe the employment-at-will doctrine.

1-2. Explain the implied-contract exception to employment at will.

1-3.   Explain the covenant-of-good-faith exception to employment at will.

Educational Objective 2
Summarize the laws prohibiting discrimination on the basis of each of the following:

- **Age**
- **Sex, race, color, religion, or national origin**
- **Disability**
- **Other factors**

Key Words and Phrases

Employment at will

Bona fide occupational qualification (BFOQ)

Disparate treatment theory

Disparate impact theory

Quid pro quo sexual harassment

Hostile work environment

Affirmative action plan

Review Questions

2-1. Compare how the Age Discrimination in Employment Act (ADEA) and the Older Workers Benefit Protection Act (OWBPA) protect workers from age discrimination.

2-2. Describe the bases for discrimination covered by the Civil Rights Act of 1964 and employment discrimination actions protected under Title VII of the act.

2-3. Explain how the Americans with Disabilities Act (ADA) defines the employees who are protected by the act.

Educational Objective 3

Summarize the laws governing labor-management relations in terms of the following:

- **Collective-bargaining relationships**
- **Collective-bargaining process**
- **Economic pressures**

Key Words and Phrases

Collective bargaining

Arbitration

Review Questions

3-1. Describe the two purposes of the National Labor Relations Board (NLRB).

3-2. Explain when collective bargaining is mandatory.

3-3. Compare tactics of economic pressure an employer or a union can use if there is no agreement on a contract after good-faith bargaining.

Educational Objective 4

Summarize the laws that protect employees' rights in the following areas:

- **Employee safety and health**
- **Employee wages and hours**
- **Family medical leave**
- **Employee benefits**
- **Employee privacy**

Key Words and Phrases

Occupational Safety and Health Act of 1970 (OSH Act)

Nonexempt employee

Exempt employee

Review Questions

4-1. Describe the purpose and role of the Occupational Safety and Health Administration (OSHA).

4-2. Explain the criteria for employers and employees to be covered by the Family Medical Leave Act (FMLA).

4-3. Describe requirements for insurers under the Health Insurance Portability and Accountability Act (HIPAA).

Educational Objective 5

When contemplating incorporation, explain how each of the following would factor into the decision:

- **Advantages of incorporation**
- **Federal and state regulation of corporations**
- **Foreign corporations**
- **Incorporation process**
- **Corporate ownership**

Key Words and Phrases

Pierce the corporate veil

Bond

Common stock

Preferred stock

Par value

Treasury stock

Inside director

Outside director

Review Questions

5-1. Discuss the advantages of incorporation.

5-2. Explain how corporations raise funds.

5-3. Compare corporate board of director decisions that require stockholder approval with those that do not require stockholder approval.

5-4. Describe how a corporation reacquires issued securities and reasons a corporation might choose to repurchase stock.

Educational Objective 6

Explain the rights, duties, powers, obligations, and liabilities of a corporation and the corporation's directors, officers, and stockholders.

Key Words and Phrases

Ultra vires

Derivative suit

▶▶

Review Questions

6-1. Explain the duties imposed on corporate officers and directors by the Employee Retirement Income Security Act (ERISA).

6-2. Compare the three types of civil lawsuits stockholders may file to pursue complaints.

6-3. Describe the different types of dividends that can be paid to stockholders by a corporation.

Educational Objective 7

Describe the procedures by which corporate existence can terminate through merger, dissolution, and reorganization.

Key Words and Phrases

Takeover

Tender offer

Review Questions

7-1. Describe a corporate merger.

7-2. Compare share exchange and *de facto* mergers.

7-3. Explain how one corporation may take over another corporation that does not wish to merge.

7-4. Contrast voluntary and involuntary corporate dissolution.

Educational Objective 8

Describe the characteristics, purposes, and functions of the following:

- **Partnerships**
- **Limited partnerships**
- **Limited liability partnerships**
- **Limited liability companies**

Key Words and Phrases

Partnership

Common name statute

Limited partnership

Limited liability partnership

Limited liability company (LLC)

Review Questions

8-1. Describe how partnerships form and an advantage to forming a partnership.

8-2. Explain partnership by estoppel.

8-3. Contrast rightful and wrongful dissolution of a partnership.

Application Question

8-4. Assume that Jose and Miguel form a partnership with start-up capital of
$100,000. Jose contributes $80,000 in cash, and Miguel contributes $20,000.
Miguel has advanced skills in computer systems that are essential to the business.

  a. In the first year of business, the partnership makes a $20,000 profit. How
much are Jose and Miguel each entitled to? There are no special provisions
in the partnership agreement.

b. During the third year of business, Jose and Miguel decide to dissolve the partnership. A sum of $80,000 remains after all liabilities have been paid. How much would Jose and Miguel each receive?

Educational Objective 9
Describe the characteristics, purpose, and functions of unincorporated associations.

Key Word or Phrase

Unincorporated association

Review Questions

9-1. Describe unincorporated associations.

    a. Compare associations with corporations.

    b. Compare associations with partnerships.

9-2. Describe the six major types of unincorporated associations.

9-3. Describe the liability of association members to third parties.

   a. Contrast the liability for contracts made by for-profit associations with those made by not-for-profit associations.

   b. Contrast the liability of association members for actions of employees and the actions of those performing voluntary services.

9-4. Describe how associations can be dissolved.

Answers to Assignment 9 Questions

NOTE: These answers are provided to give students a basic understanding of acceptable types of responses. They often are not the only valid answers and are not intended to provide an exhaustive response to the questions.

Educational Objective 1

1-1. Under the traditional common law doctrine of employment at will, in the absence of an express contract or union collective bargaining agreement stating otherwise, an employer is free to terminate any employee at any time, for any reason or for no reason at all.

1-2. An implied contract may exist if the terms and intentions of employment are indicated by the actions of the parties and the surrounding circumstances, rather than expressly written. For example, an employee handbook or supervisor's statement that an employee may be fired only for "just cause" might be interpreted as an implied contract that prohibits termination without cause.

1-3. The covenant-of-good-faith exception, also called the implied-in-law contract exception, creates a broad exception to employment at will. Under this exception, the employer has an obligation because of a special relationship with the employee or the conduct of the parties. For example, an employer could be found to have operated in bad faith for terminating a long-term employee just before that employee became eligible for retirement benefits.

Educational Objective 2

2-1. The ADEA prohibits discrimination, on the basis of age, against persons age forty or older. This act extends the prohibition to all aspects of employment, including hiring, pay, terms, conditions, privileges, and termination. The OWBPA has a narrower scope than the ADEA and specifically prohibits age discrimination in the offering of benefits.

2-2. The Civil Rights Act of 1964 expanded the bases of discrimination of race, color, and national origin to include sex and religion. Title VII of the act governs most employment discrimination actions, including pregnancy discrimination, sexual discrimination (including sexual harassment), and sex-based insurance rates.

2-3. The employees who are protected by the ADA are defined as qualified individuals with a disability who, with or without reasonable accommodation, can perform the essential functions of the job. A disability includes any physical or mental impairment that substantially limits one or more of the major life activities of an individual.

Educational Objective 3

3-1. Created by Congress as part of the National Labor Relations Act (NLRA), the NLRB has a two-fold purpose. The first purpose is to prevent and remedy unfair labor practices, whether conducted by labor organizations or by employers. The second purpose is to determine whether or not certain groups of employees desire labor organization representation, and their selection of a union, for collective-bargaining purposes.

3-2. Collective bargaining is mandatory for wages, hours, and other terms of employment. Any issue relating to an aspect of the relationship between the employer and employee is considered an issue requiring mandatory bargaining.

3-3. The tactics of economic pressure a union can use include a strike, boycott, or picketing. The tactics of economic pressure an employer can use include using replacement employees or, under certain conditions, a lockout, when the employer withholds work from the employees.

Educational Objective 4

4-1. Congress created OSHA to enforce the Occupational Safety and Health Act (OSH Act). OSHA is responsible for issuing and modifying the occupational safety and health standards applicable to businesses. OSHA also has the responsibility to conduct workplace inspections; to investigate complaints regarding working conditions; and to issue regulations requiring employers to record and report certain work-related injuries, illness, or deaths.

4-2. The FMLA applies to employers who have fifty or more employees (including full-time, part-time, and temporary workers) during at least twenty weeks in the current or preceding year, located within a seventy-five mile radius of the work location where the employee requests leave. The FMLA applies to employees who have worked for an employer subject to FMLA requirements for at least twelve months (not necessary consecutive) and for at least 1,250 hours during the twelve-month period preceding the leave.

4-3. Under the Health Insurance Portability and Accountability Act (HIPAA), healthcare providers, health plans, and other healthcare services must adhere to guidelines established by the statute. The act grants all patients the right to see, copy, and request to amend their own medical records. Notice of privacy practices about how a patient's medical information is used and disclosed must be given to the patient by each medical professional or medical facility. Medical information must be protected and not disclosed except as permitted by law.

Educational Objective 5

5-1. The primary advantage of incorporation is that it limits the owners' liability for the corporation's contracts and torts. Other possible advantages include tax advantages, ease in sale or transfer ownership, ease in raising capital, and perpetuity beyond the death of owners.

5-2. Corporations raise funds by issuing two principal types of securities: debt securities and equity securities. A debt security, or bond, is a debt obligation. Equity securities are the corporation's capital stock and represent the stockholders' ownership of and equity, or financial interest, in the corporation. Bondholders are the creditors of the corporation, while stockholders are owners of the corporation.

5-3. Board decisions that would change the terms of the contract between the corporation and its stockholders require stockholder approval. Examples of such decisions include amendments to the articles of incorporation (including capital structure, purpose, name, or preemptive right limitations), mergers or consolidation, and dissolution of the corporation. Board decisions regarding business policy do not usually require stockholder approval. These decisions include issuing stock, borrowing money, electing and assigning officer duties, declaring dividends, purchasing or selling property in the normal course of business, decisions concerning insurance coverage, and general policy decisions regarding company operations.

5-4. A corporation may reacquire issued securities by repurchasing them. This reacquisition is known as redemption. The original agreements between the corporation and the purchasers of debt securities and preferred stock can include provisions to make the securities redeemable at the corporation's option or to provide for a mandatory retirement of the security. A corporation may provide for redemption of nonvoting stock but cannot provide for the redemption of all common voting stock. A corporation can redeem stock only if its assets exceed its liabilities, including any obligations to preferred stockholders in the event of dissolution.

One reason a corporation may choose to repurchase stock is that a reduction in the number of issued shares may result in a stronger return on investment. If earnings are static, the earnings per share will increase with fewer outstanding shares. Another reason is that repurchasing shares can make a corporation less attractive for a takeover. Stock repurchases can reduce accumulation of excessive cash in the corporation and increase the market value of remaining outstanding stock. Both of these are deterrents to a takeover.

Educational Objective 6

6-1. A director or an officer who exercises discretionary control in the management or assets of a corporation's pension or health benefit plan is a fiduciary under ERISA with specific statutory duties and liabilities. Directors and officers have duties to act solely in the plan participants' interest, to exercise the care and skill of a reasonable person conducting a similar enterprise, to diversify investments unless it is clearly unreasonable to do so, and to act in accordance with the plan documents.

6-2. Stockholders may file a class action suit when a transaction damages multiple stockholders. A common example is a stockholder class action suit against directors and officers for damages for fraud, such as failure to make a full disclosure in connection with a public stock offering. An individual stockholder might file suit to seek a remedy for direct harm, such as an injury sustained while engaged in company business. The third type of lawsuit is filed on behalf of the corporation itself by one or more stockholders, and this type of lawsuit is a derivative action. For example, stockholders might file a derivative suit if an outside auditing firm negligently audited the books of the corporation.

6-3. Dividends come from corporate profits. Cash dividends are the type most frequently paid by corporations. Property dividends are shares of another corporation that the declaring corporation has acquired. Stock dividends are corporate profits issued in the form of additional shares of the issuing corporation. Stock dividends are paid either in treasury stock or from authorized but unissued shares. An extra dividend is a dividend in addition to the usual and expected regular dividend. A liquidating dividend is not a true dividend because it does not come from corporate profit, and it is a distribution of assets during a corporate reorganization.

Educational Objective 7

7-1. In a corporate merger, two or more corporations join to become a new, single corporation. The newly merged corporation owns all the assets and is subject to all the liabilities of the merging corporations. A true merger is considered a friendly transaction to which the boards of both (or all) merging organizations agree.

7-2. In a share exchange merger, a corporation acquires all of another corporation's outstanding shares in return for shares of the acquiring corporation. A *de facto* merger occurs when one corporation sells all or most of its assets to another corporation, in return for the purchasing corporation's shares, for distribution to its stockholders.

7-3. The acquiring corporation can attempt a hostile takeover. This can be accomplished by making a tender offer for shareholders' stock and thus acquiring sufficient stock to become eligible to vote on the board of directors. A takeover can also be accomplished by the acquiring corporation's obtaining sufficient proxies from the unwilling target corporation's stockholders (often by proposing a higher share price than the one at which the stock currently trades) for the acquiring corporation to elect its own board of directors or to vote for a merger.

7-4. Voluntary corporate dissolution begins with a board resolution to dissolve the corporation, approved by a majority of the stockholders. The corporation files a "statement of intent to dissolve" with the state and then proceeds with liquidation. Involuntary dissolution occurs when the state of incorporation, the stockholders, or corporate creditors file for involuntary dissolution proceedings.

Educational Objective 8

8-1. Partnerships can arise by people's actions as partners, by oral agreement, or by written agreement. Two or more persons are presumed to be partners if they agree to work together in any line of activity and share the profits and losses, although not necessarily on an equal basis. To be considered a partnership, the enterprise need not have physical assets but must have profit as its goal. An advantage of forming a partnership is that income is taxable at each individual partner's tax rate rather than at a rate that would apply to a corporation.

8-2. A partnership by estoppel results if three elements are present. First, a person who is not a partner acts as if he or she is a partner or permits others to think he or she is a partner. Second, a third party deals with the entity in justifiable reliance on a belief that it is a partnership or that the person who claims to be a partner is actually a partner. Third, the third party changes his or her legal position because of reliance on that belief, such as entering into a contract. Under these circumstances, the person who has permitted the appearance is liable to the third party to the same extent that an actual partner would be. In addition, the presumed partner has the power to bind the partnership, just as an actual partner would.

8-3. A rightful dissolution of a partnership is one that is in accordance with the partnership agreement and is not any partner's fault. On rightful dissolution, the partnership is liquidated and assets distributed. Wrongful dissolution of a partnership occurs when there is fault on the part of one or more partners. The innocent partners can either liquidate the business or continue the business for the remainder of the partnership term. If they choose to continue, the remaining partners must pay the wrongful partner his or her share of the assets, less any damages the wrongful dissolution caused.

8-4. These answers are based on the facts presented about Jose and Miguel's partnership:

a. Jose and Miguel are each entitled to a $10,000 profit.

b. The partnership has a $20,000 loss ($100,000 initial capital – $80,000 assets remaining). Jose is entitled to $70,000 (his initial investment of $80,000 – half of the $20,000 loss). Miguel would receive $10,000 (his initial investment of $20,000 – half of the $20,000 loss).

Educational Objective 9

9-1. Unincorporated associations are formed under the common law right of contract, have no separate legal existence, and do not legally possess perpetual life.

  a. Associations, although unincorporated, resemble corporations in their form and organization. An association typically has a contract of association similar to a corporate charter. The biggest difference between a corporation and an association is that an association is not a legal entity separate from its members and managers. Associations are not subject to franchise, transfer, and other taxes commonly levied on corporations. Unlike corporations, associations do not need to register in the states in which they do business or file various reports required of corporations.

  b. An association resembles a partnership in that, because an association is not a separate legal entity like a corporation, its members may be individually liable for the association's activities. Associations differ from partnerships in several ways. An association, unlike a partnership, cannot usually hold title to real property or execute a lease in the association's name. A member's withdrawal does not cause dissolution of an association as it would in a partnership. Any expense-sharing or profit-sharing in an association is frequently other than per capita. An association's individual members do not have the authority that partners do to participate directly in its day-to-day management.

9-2. These are the six major types of unincorporated associations:

  • Trade associations foster their members' interests by exchanging and compiling information, lobbying, setting standards, and issuing publicity. Trade associations form the largest group of unincorporated associations.

  • Labor unions are the second largest group of associations. Local unions, as well as national organizations representing multiple smaller unions, may be formed as associations.

  • Benevolent and fraternal associations have traditionally taken the form of associations. If these organizations provide insurance or credit for their members, they must comply with state laws governing such issues.

  • Religious organizations may be unincorporated associations, although they may choose to incorporate.

  • Clubs are associations of persons for some common objective, such as social purposes.

  • Condominium owners' associations are usually regulated by state statutes. All unit owners within the condominium are association members, and the association is responsible for the condominium's operation and the care and preservation of the common areas.

9-3.   Individual members can be liable for both torts and contracts arising from the association's activities. Even in states that now allow unincorporated associations to sue and be sued, the possibility of the association being sued does not eliminate the members' individual liability.

   a.   Absent statutes to the contrary, members of an association organized for trade or profit are individually liable for contracts made by an authorized officer or agent in the association's name or incurred in the course of business for which the association was organized. This liability exists even if the other party does not know the individual members' names. Members of not-for-profit associations, however, do not have individual liability to third parties unless they join in authorizing a contract.

   b.   Association members are jointly and severally liable for torts committed by the association's agents and employees acting within the scope of their employment. However, under the Volunteer Protection Act, those who provide voluntary services are immune from liability in many instances.

9-4.   Because no specific statutory provisions apply to the dissolution of associations, they can be dissolved in a variety of ways. Associations can be dissolved by members' vote; by the death or withdrawal of a majority of the members; by court action on application of creditors or members, or for illegal conduct; and by the expiration of a period stated in the articles.

Direct Your Learning

The International Legal Environment

Educational Objectives

After learning the content of this assignment, you should be able to:

1. Describe each of the methods a company can use to engage in international business, including key issues involved in each method:

   - Foreign trade

   - Foreign contractual relationships

   - Foreign direct investments

2. Describe the characteristics of these predominant legal systems:

   - Civil law (including Roman-French, German, and Scandinavian)

   - Common law

   - East Asian

   - Hindu

   - Islamic

   - Socialist-Communist

3. Distinguish between public international law and private international law.

4. Summarize the roles and/or responsibilities of these multinational organizations and agreements in influencing the direction and development of world business:

   - United Nations

   - World Trade Organization

   - The North American Free Trade Agreement

   - European Union

   - Association of Southeast Asian Nations

10

- Asia-Pacific Economic Cooperation

5. Explain how a U.S. company's international business can be affected by these U.S. laws:

   - Internal Revenue Code

   - Foreign Corrupt Practices Act

   - Patriot Act

6. Explain how each of the following financial considerations can affect a company engaged in international business:

   - Currency and foreign exchange markets

   - Expropriation

   - Accounting standards

   - Taxation

   - Tax havens

7. Describe these factors affecting companies involved in international business:

   - Language

   - Culture

   - Time differences

   - Distance and space

   - Types of government

Outline

▶ **Methods of Engaging in International Business**
  A. Foreign Trade
    1. Export Controls
    2. Import Controls
    3. International Sales Contracts
    4. Selling Terms
    5. Methods of Payment
  B. Foreign Contractual Relationships
    1. Product Licensing
    2. Franchising
  C. Foreign Direct Investment
    1. Subsidiaries
    2. Joint Ventures

▶ **Legal Systems**
  A. Civil Law
    1. Roman-French Law
    2. German Law
    3. Scandinavian Law
  B. Common Law
  C. East Asian Law
  D. Hindu Law
  E. Islamic Law
  F. Socialist-Communist Law

▶ **International Law**
  A. Public International Law
  B. Private International Law

▶ **Multinational Organizations and Agreements**
  A. United Nations (UN)
    1. General Assembly
    2. Security Council
    3. Economic and Social Council
    4. International Court of Justice
    5. Secretariat
  B. World Trade Organization (WTO)
  C. North American Free Trade Agreement (NAFTA)
  D. European Union (EU)
  E. Association of Southeast Asian Nations (ASEAN)

  F. Asia-Pacific Economic Cooperation (APEC)

▶ **United States Laws Affecting International Business**
  A. Tax Code
  B. Foreign Corrupt Practices Act
  C. The Patriot Act

▶ **Financial Considerations in International Business**
  A. Currency and Foreign Exchange Markets
    1. Supply and Demand
    2. International Assets
  B. Expropriation
  C. Accounting Standards
  D. Taxation
  E. Tax Havens
    1. Types of Corporate Tax Structures
    2. Information Privacy

▶ **Non-Legal Factors Affecting International Business**
  A. Language
  B. Culture
  C. Time Differences
  D. Distance and Space
  E. Types of Government

Perform a final review before your exam, but don't cram. Give yourself between two and four hours to go over the course work.

For each assignment, you should define or describe each of the Key Words and Phrases and answer each of the Review and Application Questions.

Educational Objective 1

Describe each of the methods a company can use to engage in international business, including key issues involved in each method:

- **Foreign trade**
- **Foreign contractual relationships**
- **Foreign direct investments**

Key Word or Phrase

Business risk

Review Questions

1-1. Describe the key issues related to regulatory compliance and sales contracts for organizations involved in foreign trade.

1-2. Explain how insurers participating in worldwide insurance markets can insure global risks without violating United States sanctions laws.

1-3. Explain how licensing is used to regulate goods imported into the U.S.

1-4. Explain how the United Nations Convention of Contracts for the International Sale of Goods (CISG) facilitates international trade.

1-5. Distinguish between the open account and letter of credit methods of payment.

1-6. Explain how a domestic firm considering granting a product license to a foreign firm can protect its assets.

1-7. Identify an important aspect of franchising as a method of conducting international business.

Educational Objective 2

Describe the characteristics of these predominant legal systems:

- **Civil law (including Roman-French, German, and Scandinavian)**
- **Common law**
- **East Asian**
- **Hindu**
- **Islamic**
- **Socialist-Communist**

Review Questions

2-1. Identify the two major legal systems.

2-2. Name the three stages of a typical civil-law case.

2-3. Describe the common-law legal system.

2-4. Explain why private-sector business legal principles, such as contracts and bankruptcy, are of little use within the socialist legal system.

Educational Objective 3
Distinguish between public international law and private international law.

Key Words and Phrases

Public international law

Private international law

Review Questions

3-1. Contrast public and private international law.

3-2. Define comity as it relates to private international law.

3-3. Explain the three areas of jurisdiction that courts in international cases must determine before presiding over a particular case.

Educational Objective 4

Summarize the roles and/or responsibilities of these multinational organizations and agreements in influencing the direction and development of world business:

- **United Nations**
- **World Trade Organization**
- **The North American Free Trade Agreement**
- **European Union**
- **Association of Southeast Asian Nations**
- **Asia-Pacific Economic Cooperation**

Key Words and Phrases

Dumping

Common Market

Review Questions

4-1. What are the purposes of the United Nations (UN)?

4-2. Identify the three primary World Trade Organization (WTO) agreements.

4-3. To what countries does the North American Free Trade Agreement (NAFTA) apply?

4-4. What effect did NAFTA have on tariffs?

4-5. Describe the two purposes of the Association of Southeast Asian Nations (ASEAN).

4-6. Describe the purpose of Asia-Pacific Economic Cooperation (APEC).

Educational Objective 5

Explain how a U.S. company's international business can be affected by these U.S. laws:

- **Internal Revenue Code**
- **Foreign Corrupt Practices Act**
- **Patriot Act**

Review Questions

5-1. What is repatriation of earnings?

5-2. Describe the characteristics of the Foreign Corrupt Practices Act (FCPA).

5-3. Explain how the following sections of the Patriot Act affect businesses:

  a. Section 215

  b. Subtitle B (Sections 351-366)

  c. Section 352

Educational Objective 6

Explain how each of the following financial considerations can affect a company engaged in international business:

- **Currency and foreign exchange markets**
- **Expropriation**
- **Accounting standards**
- **Taxation**
- **Tax havens**

Key Words and Phrases

Pegged currency

Transfer price

Tax haven

Bearer share

Registered share

Review Questions

6-1. Identify situations in which currency can lose value relative to other currencies.

6-2. What are the financial considerations in the international insurance market?

6-3. Contrast expropriation and eminent domain.

6-4. Identify the different approaches to taxing a corporation's earnings in the context of international commerce.

6-5. What should a business consider when establishing a subsidiary in an offshore tax haven?

6-6. Identify the four types of corporate tax structures that a tax haven country may have.

Educational Objective 7

Describe these factors affecting companies involved in international business:

- **Language**
- **Culture**
- **Time differences**
- **Distance and space**
- **Types of government**

Key Words and Phrases

Democratic rule

Nonparty democracy

Parliamentary democracy

Presidential democracy

Multiparty democracy

Junta

Martial law

Monarchy

Absolute monarchy

Constitutional monarchy

Single-party government

Theocratic government

Transitional government

Review Questions

7-1. Identify the challenges facing companies engaging in international business.

7-2. Describe the four forms of modern democratic government.

7-3. Contrast absolute monarchy and constitutional monarchy.

Application Question

7-4. FIC, a United States corporation, is investigating doing business in Peru and Liberia. Identify the challenges FIC might face in each of these countries.

Answers to Assignment 10 Questions

NOTE: These answers are provided to give students a basic understanding of acceptable types of responses. They often are not the only valid answers and are not intended to provide an exhaustive response to the questions.

Educational Objective 1

1-1. Export and import controls imposed by the United States government are important regulatory concerns, while international sales contract concerns include terms of sale and methods of payment.

1-2. Insurers participating in worldwide insurance markets through global insurance policies can insure global risks without violating U.S. sanctions law by inserting policy language that explicitly excludes risks violating U.S. sanctions laws.

1-3. By requiring a license to conduct business, the government ensures that goods will be imported into the country on more favorable terms than if domestic companies competed for the goods for use or resale.

1-4. CISG facilitates international trade by providing rules for writing international contracts and for the transfer of goods under the contracts.

1-5. An open account is a rotating charge account under which the buyer settles the account at determined intervals. With a letter of credit, the buyer establishes credit with a local bank, which then contacts a bank in the seller's country, establishing a credit line in favor of the seller. The seller then receives a letter of credit in confirmation of the credit.

1-6. Before entering into any agreement, the domestic company assesses the trustworthiness of the foreign company it is dealing with and the foreign company's ability to meet the financial requirements of the licensing agreement.

1-7. An important aspect of franchising is the control over the use of the company's name and the quality of the product or service.

Educational Objective 2

2-1. The two major legal systems in the majority of countries are the civil-law system and the common-law system.

2-2. The three stages of a typical civil-law case are these:

- The preliminary stage

- The evidence stage

- The decision stage

2-3. In the common-law legal system, a judge interprets the facts of a case, examines precedents, and makes a decision based on the facts in the current case.

2-4. Private-sector business legal principles, such as contracts, commercial law, torts, property, and bankruptcy, are of little use within a socialist system. Public law replaces private-sector legal principles. For example, because the government owns all property and production, all contract law is public. In a socialist country, the socialist political party controls and influences the entire legal system, including the courts. All decisions from the courts, although independent in nature, are subject to party control or revision.

Educational Objective 3

3-1. Public international law concerns the interrelation of nation states and is governed by treaties and other international agreements, while private international law involves disputes between individuals or corporations in different countries.

3-2. Comity is the practice by which one country recognizes, within its own territory or in its courts, another country's institutions.

3-3. Courts in international cases must determine whether they have jurisdiction over the person or entity (*in personam* jurisdiction) and over the subject matter (*in res* jurisdiction) and if they have jurisdiction to render the particular judgment in the case.

Educational Objective 4

4-1. The UN's purposes are these:

- To maintain international peace and security
- To develop friendly relations among nations
- To cooperate in solving international economic, social, cultural, and humanitarian problems
- To promote respect for human rights and fundamental freedoms
- To be a center for harmonizing the actions of nations in attaining these goals

4-2. The three primary WTO agreements are these:

- The General Agreement on Tariffs and Trade (GATT)
- The General Agreement on Trade in Services (GATS)
- The Agreement on Trade-Related Aspects of Intellectual Property Rights (TRIPS Agreement)

4-3. NAFTA applies to Canada, Mexico, and the United States.

4-4. NAFTA eliminated nearly all tariffs between the U.S. and Canada by 1998 and nearly all tariffs between the U.S. and Mexico by 2008.

4-5. ASEAN's purposes are twofold:

- Accelerating the economic growth, social progress, and cultural development of the region through joint endeavors in the spirit of equality and partnership to strengthen the foundation for a prosperous and peaceful community of Southeast Asian nations
- Promoting regional peace and stability through respect for justice and the rule of law in the relationship among countries in the region and adherence to the principles of the UN Charter

4-6. APEC has attempted to facilitate economic growth, cooperation, trade, and investment in the Asia-Pacific region and is the only intergovernmental body that operates on the basis of nonbinding commitments, open dialogue, and equal respect for the views of all participant countries.

Educational Objective 5

5-1. Repatriation of earnings is the process by which a U.S. parent company moves earnings from its foreign-based affiliates back to the U.S. to the parent company or its stockholders.

5-2. In general, the FCPA prohibits payments to foreign officials to obtain or keep business. Congress enacted the FCPA to stop these acts and to restore public confidence in the integrity of the U.S. business system. The FCPA also requires companies who list their securities in the U.S. to meet certain accounting provisions.

5-3. The selected sections of the Patriot Act affect businesses in these ways:

   a. Section 215 revises the Foreign Intelligence Surveillance Act (FISA) to allow the FBI to subpoena all business records for foreign intelligence and international terrorism investigations.

   b. Subtitle B (Sections 351-366) amends the banking and finance laws to permit the government access to information from banks that might relate to terrorism. Additionally, Section 351 allows the Secretary of the Treasury to impose sanctions, including cutting off all dealings with U.S. financial institutions or banks in foreign nations whose bank secrecy laws deny information to U.S. agencies.

   c. Section 352 prohibits financial institutions from knowingly becoming involved in unlawful financial transactions with suspected terrorists and requires that companies establish and maintain written, anti-money-laundering programs that, at a minimum, do the following: (1) incorporate internal policies, procedures, and controls based on the company's assessment of its money-laundering risks; (2) designate a compliance officer; and (3) establish ongoing employee-training programs as well as independent audit functions to test programs.

Educational Objective 6

6-1. A currency tends to lose value, relative to other currencies, if that country's inflation level is relatively high, if the country's level of output is expected to decline, or if a country is troubled by political uncertainty.

6-2. Financial considerations in the international insurance market include these:

   • Currency and foreign exchange markets

   • Expropriation

   • Accounting issues

   • Taxation issues

   • Tax havens

6-3. Expropriation is a government's lawful acquisition of property without the owner's consent and often without fair compensation. The government acquires property rights and the owner loses them. Eminent domain is a government's power to confiscate private property for public use. The U.S. Constitution requires just compensation for property taken by eminent domain.

6-4. The different approaches to taxing a corporation's earnings in the context of international commerce are these:

- Territorial tax systems

- Worldwide tax system

- Border tax adjustments

- Earnings stripping

- Inversion (or expatriation, or reincorporation)

6-5. A business should consider these factors when establishing a subsidiary in an offshore tax haven:

- The country's tax structure

- The country's level of enforcement of its privacy laws

- The country's language

- The type of judicial system in the country

- The country's political stability

- The country's independence from the parent company's home country

- The costs of establishing the new subsidiary in the country

6-6. A tax haven country may have one of these four types of corporate tax structures:

- Low or minimum taxes

- No corporate taxes

- No taxes on foreign income

- Special tax concessions

Educational Objective 7

7-1. The challenges facing companies engaging in international business include the language barrier, cultural differences, time differences between countries, physical distance and space between countries, and government structure.

7-2. These are the four forms of modern democratic government:

- A nonparty democracy is a form of government in which elected representatives have no political party affiliation.

- A parliamentary democracy is ruled by a prime minister and an elected parliament.

- A presidential democracy is governed by a president directly elected by the citizens.

- A multiparty democracy is a form of government in which representatives may be elected from several or many political parties.

7-3. In an absolute monarchy, the leader rules alone and selects advisers for assistance. In a constitutional monarchy, a parliament, or democratic legislative body, replaces absolute monarchical rule.

7-4. In Peru, FIC could face these challenges: language, culture, and physical distance and space. Time differences probably would not be a problem because Peru is in a similar time zone.

In Liberia, FIC could face these challenges: distance and space, culture, and time differences. The company should research what language problems might arise as well as the stability of the form of government.

Exam Information

About Institutes Exams

Exam questions are based on the Educational Objectives stated in the course guide and textbook. The exam is designed to measure whether you have met those Educational Objectives. The exam does not necessarily test every Educational Objective. It tests over a balanced sample of Educational Objectives.

How to Prepare for Institutes Exams

What can you do to prepare for an Institutes exam? Students who pass Institutes exams do the following:

▶ Use the assigned study materials. Focus your study on the Educational Objectives presented at the beginning of each course guide assignment. Thoroughly read the textbook and any other assigned materials, and then complete the course guide exercises. Choose a study method that best suits your needs; for example, participate in a traditional class, online class, or informal study group; or study on your own. Use The Institutes' SMART Study Aids (if available) for practice and review. If this course has an associated SMART Online Practice Exams product, you will find an access code on the inside back cover of this course guide. This access code allows you to print a full practice exam and to take additional online practice exams that will simulate an actual credentialing exam.

▶ Become familiar with the types of test questions asked on the exam. The practice exam in this course guide or in the SMART Online Practice Exams product will help you understand the different types of questions you will encounter on the exam.

▶ Maximize your test-taking time. Successful students use the sample exam in the course guide or in the SMART Online Practice Exams product to practice pacing themselves. Learning how to manage your time during the exam ensures that you will complete all of the test questions in the time allotted.

Types of Exam Questions

The exam for this course consists of objective questions of several types.

The Correct-Answer Type

In this type of question, the question stem is followed by four responses, one of which is absolutely correct. Select the *correct* answer.

> Which one of the following persons evaluates requests for insurance to deter-mine which applicants are accepted and which are rejected?
>
> a.   The premium auditor
>
> b.   The loss control representative
>
> c.   The underwriter
>
> d.   The risk manager

The Best-Answer Type

In this type of question, the question stem is followed by four responses, only one of which is best, given the statement made or facts provided in the stem. Select the *best* answer.

> Several people within an insurer might be involved in determining whether an applicant for insurance is accepted. Which one of the following positions is primarily responsible for determining whether an applicant for insurance is accepted?
>
> a.   The loss control representative
>
> b.   The customer service representative
>
> c.   The underwriter
>
> d.   The premium auditor

The Incomplete-Statement or Sentence-Completion Type

In this type of question, the last part of the question stem consists of a portion of a statement rather than a direct question. Select the phrase that *correctly* or *best* completes the sentence.

> Residual market plans designed for individuals who are unable to obtain insurance on their personal property in the voluntary market are called
>
> a. VIN plans.
>
> b. Self-insured retention plans.
>
> c. Premium discount plans.
>
> d. FAIR plans.

"All of the Above" Type

In this type of question, only one of the first three answers could be correct, or all three might be correct, in which case the best answer would be "All of the above." Read all the answers and select the *best* answer.

> When a large commercial insured's policy is up for renewal, who is likely to provide input to the renewal decision process?
>
> a. The underwriter
>
> b. The loss control representative
>
> c. The producer
>
> d. All of the above

"All of the following, EXCEPT:" Type

In this type of question, responses include three correct answers and one answer that is incorrect or is clearly the least correct. Select the *incorrect* or *least correct* answer.

> All of the following adjust insurance claims, EXCEPT:
>
> a. Insurer claims representatives
>
> b. Premium auditors
>
> c. Producers
>
> d. Independent adjusters

About the Code of Professional Conduct

This is a brief summary of information appearing in greater detail in the CPCU Code of Professional Conduct.

All CPCU candidates and CPCUs are bound by the CPCU Code of Professional Conduct. The Code describes both high goals and minimum standards of conduct.

- The high goals described in the Canons challenge all CPCUs and CPCU candidates to aspire to the highest level of ethical performance in all of their professional activities.
- The minimum standards of conduct, described in the Rules, maintain the integrity of the CPCU designation. CPCUs and CPCU candidates are obligated to at least meet the minimum standards in the Rules, and failure to do so may subject a CPCU—or a CPCU candidate—to disciplinary measures.

In the process of satisfying the ethics requirement, CPCU candidates study the Code and are tested to ensure that all CPCUs understand their ethical obligations. The ultimate goal of the Code is to foster highly ethical conduct on the part of all CPCUs.

The CPCU Code of Professional Conduct Canons

Canon 1—Insurance professionals should endeavor to place the public interest above their own.

Canon 2—Insurance professionals should seek continually to maintain and improve their professional knowledge, skills, and competence.

Canon 3—Insurance professionals should obey all laws and regulations, and should avoid any conduct or activity that would cause unjust harm to others.

Canon 4—Insurance professionals should be diligent in the performance of their occupational duties and should continually strive to improve the functioning of the insurance mechanism.

Canon 5—Insurance professionals should aspire to raise the professional and ethical standards in the insurance business.

Canon 6—Insurance professionals should strive to establish and maintain dignified and honorable relationships with those whom they serve, with fellow insurance practitioners, and with members of other professions.

Canon 7—Insurance professionals should assist in improving the public understanding of insurance and risk management.

Canon 8—CPCUs should honor the integrity of the CPCU designation and respect the limitations placed on its use.

Canon 9—CPCUs should assist in maintaining the integrity of the CPCU Code of Professional Conduct.